FISH FLORIDA
SALTWATER

Boris Arnov

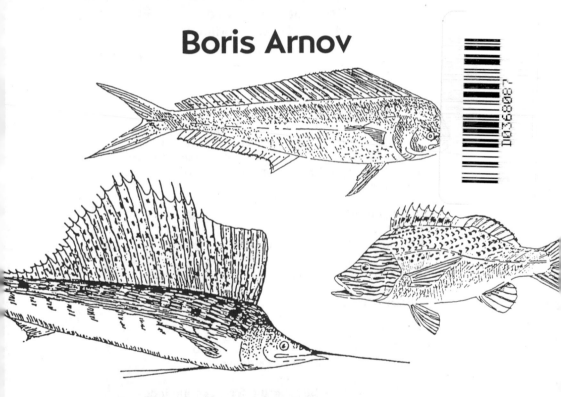

Illustrations by Susan Jyl Feldmann

Gulf Publishing Company
Houston, Texas

For my mother and the memory of all our
fishing together.

> This edition reviewed
> by the author and reprinted
> February 1998.

Gulf Publishing Company
Book Division
P.O. Box 2608, Houston, Texas 77252-2608

10   9   8   7   6   5

Library of Congress Cataloging-in-Publication Data

Arnov, Boris.
    Fish Florida:saltwater/by Boris Arnov;
  illustrations by Susan Jyl Feldmann.
        p.   cm.
    Includes bibliographical references and index.
    ISBN 0-88415-002-X
    1. Saltwater fishing—Florida—Guide-books.
    2. Florida—Description and travel—1981—Guide-
  books.   I. Feldmann, Susan Jyl.   II. Title.
  SH483.A76   1991
  799.1′6′09759—dc20   91-4793
                                               CIP

Contents

— Mackerels —

— Marlins —

Introduction

This guide tells how, when, and where to catch the saltwater game fishes of Florida. As with any book containing this sort of information, the reader should realize that ten anglers asked the same fishing question will respond with ten different answers. Therefore, be warned! There are other ways, times, and locations not in this guide that catch fish, but what is here has worked very well for many fishermen and women for many years. So start with the information in this guide, but always follow up with advice from a local bait and tackle store for what is important to know *at that moment.*

Some readers might wonder why certain fishes have been left out. Swordfish, for example, are not given a special chapter because commercial fishermen have nearly wiped them out, and it would mislead a reader to see a section on such a fish. Likewise with spearfish: They are so rare that you may fish a lifetime and never see one. This simply means that the fishes covered in this guide are there for the catching now.

Others might wonder why their favorite fish receives unequal treatment compared with some others. Because some fishes such as the sailfish and spotted seatrout have been fishing targets for a long time, the angling methods are diverse and sophisticated and require more space to describe. The angler should, therefore, read the entire chapter on the fish he or she seeks, because information found for one type of fishing, such as trolling, might be useful for another, such as casting.

Another example of a question a reader might raise is why tripletail fishing around weed in the Atlantic Ocean is not described. The reason is that only the best fishing areas for each species—not all areas where the fish is found—have been included. This means that even though bonefish have been caught in the northeastern part of Florida, the sensible angler would never seek them there instead of the Keys.

Regarding fishing times recommended, the thoughtful fisherman will realize that sailfish, for example, might be caught in the Gulf Stream off Jacksonville in the winter, but he will find no mention of this in the guide, because fishing fifty miles offshore during the stormy months of the year is not the safest procedure. So, for a variety of reasons, only the best times to fish are recommended even though fish can be caught at other times as well.

When a rig or knot is mentioned, the fisherman will find it illustrated and explained in the appendix of the book. The tackle, rigs, and directions about how to prepare baits are methods that have worked for a long time. This does not mean that something different will not catch fish—try it. Also, even though a certain size fly rod, for example, is recommended for sailfish, you must consider whether this is a sensible pursuit, not only whether it is possible or not. Outside of being very expensive in terms of equipment and personnel required, fighting a large fish for a long time on super-light tackle stresses the fish so much that should one wish to release it, survival is doubtful.

When it comes to artificial baits, there are many more on the market than are mentioned in these pages. One can easily accumulate hundreds of dollars worth of casting plugs. Those recommended in the guide are known to catch fish, but there are many others locally used that might work as well or better. Before buying, check with fishermen as well as fishing tackle stores.

Regulations about Florida fishing have often changed over the past few years. The one dependable fact is the necessity of having the new saltwater fishing license. About the only persons exempt are Florida residents who fish from land or bridges and piers, anyone fishing from a guided boat, youngsters under 16, and anglers 65 and older who have a Florida driver's license. Any other regulation found in the guide such as daily bag limits per person or legal sizes should be double-checked as such rules constantly change. During closed seasons, it is legal to catch and release fishes.

Another important point: If it is true that the earth is undergoing a changing weather pattern and that higher temperatures are going to be with us for a while, this will, of course, affect the when's and where's found in this guide. By the same token, if a particularly severe winter should strike, fish that usually begin to bite in March may delay until April. Again, check locally to determine current conditions.

Finally, for good fishing luck the most important act an angler can perform is to release all fish that will not be eaten and to kill only what he can use immediately. Releasing fish to resume their important role in the food chain, to breed and produce more fish, and to be there for people to catch again is the way to bring good luck.

Boris Arnov
Boca Raton, Florida

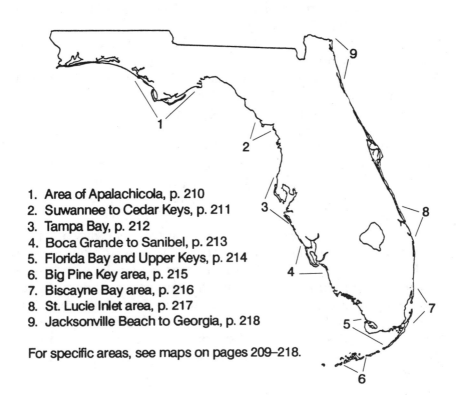

1. Area of Apalachicola, p. 210
2. Suwannee to Cedar Keys, p. 211
3. Tampa Bay, p. 212
4. Boca Grande to Sanibel, p. 213
5. Florida Bay and Upper Keys, p. 214
6. Big Pine Key area, p. 215
7. Biscayne Bay area, p. 216
8. St. Lucie Inlet area, p. 217
9. Jacksonville Beach to Georgia, p. 218

For specific areas, see maps on pages 209–218.

Amberjack; Greater Amberjack
(Seriola dumerili)

An extremely strong and hard-fighting fish that is the largest member of the jack family. Although amberjacks are used as food, there is strong evidence that some may cause ciguatera poisoning, an often fatal illness. Preferred water temperature: 65°-80° F. All-tackle record: 155 lb 10 oz.

WHERE AND WHEN

1. Atlantic coast, especially the southern part. Nearly always found around wrecks, artificial and natural reefs, and deep ledges, amberjack fishing is best from early spring to the end of May.
2. Gulf coast, especially the Panhandle. Fish are on the reefs from late February until summer warms the water and, as above, can be found around bottom structure.
3. Keys, especially the Hump, a steep rise of the ocean floor off Islamorada Key and wrecks along the 10-fathom line and deeper. Other locations are south of Key West on the Atlantic side and in the Gulf north and northwest of this city. Although year-round fishing for amberjack is possible, spring is the best time.

TACKLE

Spinning and Plug Casting. A 6'-7' rod; 15#-20# line, mono or braided; spin or conventional reel.

Deep Jigging. A stand-up rod about 5½' that has a stiff tip; 30#-50# line, mono or braided; conventional reel.

Fly. A 8½'-9' 10-12 weight rod; floating or sink-tip, weight-forward line; a reel holding at least 200 yd of 20# or heavier Dacron backing.

TECHNIQUES

Live Bait. Because amberjack are usually found deep around bottom structure, getting a live bait down to them is necessary. At such deep places as the Hump, where the fish grow very large, 6' of 100# mono attached to a strong 9/0 hook is needed. Sliding egg sinkers are placed on the line and they can add up to 16 oz, depending on the depth and amount of current. A swivel attaching line and leader keeps the lead in place. Although any live bait can be used, the torpedo-shaped, foot-long speedo is the best. Hook any live bait just ahead of the dorsal fin and lower it to the region the depth recorder indicates fish are holding. Or, if a recorder is not on the boat, lower the bait slowly, changing depth frequently, until a strike occurs. Always approach a fishing site from the downcurrent side.

Jigging. Also done where there is good bottom structure, deep jigging is not only exciting but is very effective. Use the same size tackle as you would for live bait but attach instead a white jig weighing from 2 oz - 8 oz. Tip the jig with a piece of shrimp, a strip bait, or a strip of squid; anchor upcurrent of the selected fishing site. Let the jig sink to the bottom and rapidly retrieve it to the surface. Or jig the artificial up and down at various water levels from bottom up until fish are located.

Light Tackle Casting. When using spinning, plug casting, or fly rod, the trick is to tease amberjack from the depths to within casting distance. Lower a live bait tied to the line, using no hook.

When fish follow the bait up to where they are visible, pull it away and then drop it back to them, being careful not to let them grab it. When one or more amberjack are close enough, cast an artificial so it will be clearly seen. For spinning and plug casting outfits, use a noisy, white lure such as a large popper or loud surface plug. For fly gear, use a long (6″ or so) white or yellow streamer or a large popping bug in the same colors. Spinning and plug casting need short leaders of 50#-80# mono; for fly fishing, use a 12#-16# tippet plus a foot of 80#-100# mono as a shock leader.

How to Hook an Amberjack. This rugged fish hits hard and usually hooks itself; then it takes off with great speed, usually down deep. Setting the hook once or twice when the fish settles down can guarantee it will not pull out.

Other Fish Caught While Fishing for Amberjack. Kingfish, permit, jack crevalle, barracuda, grouper and other reef fishes.

Regulations

- Closed Season: none
- Minimum Size: 28″ from nose to fork of tail
- Maximum Size: no regulation
- Daily Bag Limit: 1

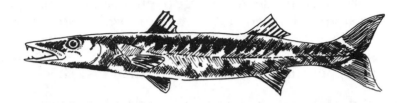

Barracuda; Great Barracuda; Cuda; Sea Pike; Giant Sea Pike
(Sphyraena barracuda)

Prized for its short but ferocious fight which often includes a magnificent jumping display, the barracuda is a favorite game fish that is often caught when fishing for something else. Small barracuda may be fair to eat but large ones definitely must be avoided as they may cause ciguatera poisoning, a possibly fatal illness in humans. Preferred water temperature: 75°–82°F. All-tackle record: 85 lb.

WHERE AND WHEN

1. All of Florida's saltwater including flats, bays, wrecks, inlets, beaches, over reefs, and near navigational markers and other structure. Although usually found in relatively shallow water, barracuda sometimes are discovered far out in the ocean as at the Rolldown, a ledge 52 miles from St. Augustine which is actually the Continental Shelf.
2. South Florida and the Keys are the warmest and therefore the most reliable place to fish for barracuda all year round. On Keys' reefs large barracuda are present in September and October and on the flats from January on. With each

passing cold front, fish can be expected to move from the reefs to the flats where they may be found either in shallow water or in pockets or holes in channels bordering flats. High tide is preferable but fish can be caught on any tide.

TACKLE

Trolling. A 20# outfit with a stand-up rod about 5½' that has about 7 guides and a conventional reel or a longer rod with a spinning reel; the capacity should be 150-200 yd.

Spinning and Plug Casting. A 6'-7' rod; 200 yd of 8#-15# line, mono or braided, the lighter being used on the flats; spin or conventional reel.

Fly. 8½'-9' 8-10 weight rod and floating line to match; reel to hold about 200 yd of 20# Dacron backing.

TECHNIQUES

Reef and Other Structure

Natural Bait. Barracuda are most often caught while fishing for some other fish and often peole can tell a barracuda is near by their odor. The smell is very much like that on a non-stainless steel knife after cutting a lemon. Trolling a swimming rather than a skipping bait is the best procedure; use a ballyhoo, mullet, or strip from a mullet or bonito. It should be double- or triple-hooked and should have 6' of #7 wire as a leader. Any small live fish hooked in any fashion will work; on a reef or a wreck it may be necessary to add weight to get the bait deep.

Artificial Bait. The dominant artificial is the tube lure, a 10"-18" piece of chartreuse, black, fluorescent red, yellow, or orange plastic through which wire runs with a treble hook at the end and sometimes with another hook protruding about the middle of the lure. The longer sizes are especially good in deeper water. Tube lures are usually cast to likely places and a ½ oz egg sinker inside the front of the plastic tube makes this possible; to go deep, 2 oz or more may be necessary. If fishing deep, allow the lure to reach bottom and then work it to the surface by varying the speed from fast to slow with plenty of hard jerks on the rod tip. If fishing a tube lure on the surface, retrieve it rapidly—the fastest retrieve possible is not too fast for a barracuda. If a fish follows but will not strike, let the lure sink a few feet and then begin to rapidly retrieve once again, adding jerks of the rod tip. In addition to tube lures, green surface plugs such as the Mirrolure 95MR, a noisy surface chugger, spoons, and deep running plugs will all pick up fish. Because of the barracuda's mouthful of sharp teeth, always use a short wire leader.

Flats

Light tackle fishing for barracuda during the winter on south Florida flats is great sport that attracts many anglers. High tide is best and you should use the same tube lure as already described but no longer than 12″. Use only the amount of weight necessary to cast and place the lure no closer than 20′ from the sighted fish; hold the rod tip high and reel in fast. If it is very calm, use a surface plug such as a noisy chugger-type. Once again, a barracuda can catch any retrieved lure, so don't be afraid to retrieve rapidly. A short piece of leader wire—about #3—is necessary.

Fly Fishing

Fly fishing for sighted barracuda is exciting and can be done on the reef where the fish frequently leap 15′ or more. Casting a fly in such a place works but it is more difficult and the sport, because it's more visual, is better when casting to sighted cudas on the flats. A leader 6′ or so with a 10#-12# tippet plus a 3″-4″ piece of #2 or #3 wire attached to the tippet with an Albright Special knot will work. Strip the following flies rapidly across the water's surface: a glass minnow tied on a 1/0 hook; the cuda fly, which is mainly about 10″ of white or chartreuse FisHair; and the Gallasch Skipping Bug, which should be worked at a speed so that it is noisy.

How to Hook a Barracuda. Very often when fishing with natural bait you will set the hook on a barracuda strike only to suddenly feel no fish on the hook—it has cut the bait off. Immediately begin jigging the rod tip rapidly; this may look like a damaged and struggling bait fish and often the barracuda returns for another mouthful.

How to Land a Barracuda. Once you have seen close-up the armament a barracuda has in its mouth, you will forever handle it with great respect. If it is a large fish, use a long-handled gaff and sink the point just behind the head, then swing the fish into the box as quickly as possible. Smaller fish can be lifted by the wire leader. However, large ones should be released because of the danger of ciguatera poisoning from eating them. The only way to safely release a large fish is to cut the wire with pliers as near to the mouth as possible, remembering that barracuda frequently choose to jump when at the boat. Smaller fish can be handled by grasping them behind the head with a gloved hand while dislodging the hook with pliers with the other hand.

Other Fish Caught While Fishing for Barracuda (on reefs and wrecks). Kingfish, amberjack, jack crevalle, and sailfish.

Regulations (none)

Black Drum; Drum; Sea Drum
(Pogonias cromis)

Drums are soft-biting fish that at first seem sluggish but quickly put up a very hard fight, pulling with great force. Small fish are fairly good to eat. Preferred water temperature: 56°-80° F. All-tackle record: 113 lb 1 oz.

WHERE AND WHEN

1. Middle to upper Atlantic coast, especially north and central coast inlets such as St. Augustine and Sebastian. Fish inlet jetties and under inlet bridges during the entire flood tide a few days on either side of a full moon. October through December are the best months and then again in March and April.
2. Middle to upper Gulf coast, especially Panhandle deep water bay mouths and Tampa Bay bridges, and John's Pass in St. Petersburg. In winter, the entire flood tide and the slack tides are the best times.

TACKLE

Bottom Fishing. Because drums grow large, hefty equipment is used to keep a hooked fish away from entangling structure. A 6′

heavy-duty rod; 40#-50# line, mono or braided; conventional reel.

Casting. A heavy casting rod seems necessary, but small jigs require a 7' rod; 20#-30# line, mono or braided; spin or conventional reel.

TECHNIQUES

Bottom-Fishing with Bait. Use a fish finder rig with enough weight to keep bait on the bottom in what is usually a swift current. A 3' 60# mono leader attached to a small hook, about a #4 or #5. Bait with one-half of a small blue crab or a small whole one with its legs and pincers removed, fiddler crabs, sand fleas, dead shrimp, live pinfish, pieces of claws, and cut-up dead fish. Try in deep holes around piers, bridge pilings, jetty rocks, etc. Chum with crushed crabs. Nighttime is best.

Casting Artificials. In the same places as above, cast a 3/8 oz grubtail jig with a black head and a motor oil colored tail.

How to Hook a Drum. Drum take the bait softly so allow the fish to carry it a short distance away before setting the hook. Time and care must be taken to land a fish this large, considering the fishing is often done over rocks.

Other Fish Caught While Fishing for Drum. Bottom fish such as snappers and occasionally bluefish and pompano, depending on the bait used.

Regulations

- Closed Season: none
- Minimum Size: 14" overall
- Maximum Size: 24" overall (one fish only this size or larger)
- Daily Bag Limit: 5
- Possession Limit: no regulation
- Note: Drums must be brought in with head and fins intact.

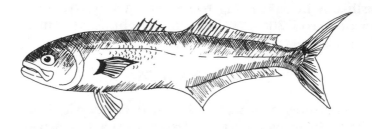

Bluefish; Blue

(Pomatomus saltatrix)

Perhaps one of the most pugnacious fishes of all, this extremely hard fighter is not reluctant to attack any bait in sight. Small blues—called snapper blues—are good to eat. Preferred water temperature: 64°-75° F. All-tackle record: 31 lb 12 oz.

WHERE AND WHEN

1. Atlantic coast beaches, all the way to the Upper Keys and Florida Bay. October to April are the best months, but blues start biting with the first north wind bringing cool weather. Caught in the surf and off fishing piers at any beach with water deep enough for schools of bait to swim close to shore, they also are taken in inlets such as at the mouth of the St. Johns River until mid-December and at inshore bodies of water near inlets, especially the Crossroads inside St. Lucie Inlet near Stuart and Lake Worth inside Lake Worth Inlet at Palm Beach. Any tide is a possibility but near a high tide and well into the outgoing tide are the best times. Early morning and before dark are generally preferable, but bluefish can go into a feeding frenzy any time of day. Onshore winds drive bait in close to shore and blues follow, often in only knee-deep water.

2. Florida Bay north to the Panhandle is a long stretch where bluefish, somewhat smaller than those in the Atlantic, are caught along the beaches, in and inside inlets all year, but perhaps best during the cool part of the year.
3. Open ocean all along the Atlantic coast to Northeast Florida, especially in March and April. These very large blues migrating north are about two miles or farther offshore in water from 120'-700', but in the northern part of the state they often show up in inlets sometime in April.

TACKLE

Spinning and Plug Casting. This equipment is primarily for inshore use and when the fish are in the surf close enough for casting. A 7' rod; 12#-15# line, mono or braided; spin or conventional reel.

Surf and Pier. Light to medium rod, 8'-14'; 25#-36# line, mono or braided; spin or conventional reel.

Ocean Trolling. A 5½' stand-up rod; 20#-30# line, mono or braided; conventional reel.

Fly. 8½'-9' 7 or 8 weight rod; weight-forward sink-tip or floating line.

TECHNIQUES

Surf and Pier

Natural Bait. Use a fish-finder rig with a 3/0 or 4/0 long-shank hook and attach it to a black swivel by means of a 1'-2' leader made of either #3 or #4 tobacco-stained stainless wire, 45# nylon-coated cable, or 50# mono; attach the swivel to the fishing line with an improved clinch knot. When the water is calm use natural bait — mullet are the best. Scale a 12" or so mullet and cut the fillets into strips 1" wide and 7" long, tapering them at the end into a point with a little flesh left attached. Thread the strip bait on the hook. Small finger mullet about 4" long are very good bait and should be used whole; hook them in the tail. It is a good idea to chum in the surf by burying the bodies of the filleted mullet in sand a few feet out into the water. Cast to feeding fish or out to the slough and reel in a few feet every few minutes.

Artificial Bait. When blues are actively feeding or when the water is rough, use artificials. In sizes from ½ oz to 2 or 3 oz, depending on the type of rig, you can use the following: Krocodile and Gator spoons; a Hopkins jig; a popper bug; a Zara Spook in red and white; a Mirrolure 77M with a dark back; a Rebel plug, large, and in black and silver.

Inlets and Inshore Water

Natural Bait. Ladyfish cut into strips 3" long and 3/4" wide threaded on a 4/0 hook are considered the best bait but mullet and menhaden are also first rate. Use a leader as above and attach it to a black swivel above which place a 1 oz egg sinker or whatever weight is necessary to get the bait to the fish.

Artificial Bait. Light tackle trolling or casting is very productive. Use a 2'-4' leader made of material described above and for a lure a Rag Mop in yellow and orange; a green tube jig; a Krocodile or Gator spoon; and a Hopkins jig.

Ocean Trolling

This is for large bluefish up to 15 lb-20 lb and appropriate tackle is necessary. Although natural bait works, it is rarely used. Tie on a 6' leader with wire, cable or mono as described above. Troll slowly and use the lures listed under surf and pier.

Fly Fishing

With a floating line for breaking fish, make a 6' leader as follows: 4' 30#, 1' 12# tippet, 4" 50#-80# mono shock for use in clear water. With sink-tip line, eliminate the 4' butt section and lengthen the tippet to about 3'; in unclear water, instead of a mono shock, make one from 3"-4" of #2 or #3 stainless wire and attach it to the rest of the leader with an Albright Special knot. Use a KA-Boom Boom Popper, 2/0; a white bucktail with a green or black back (if mullet are in the vicinity); a Lefty's Deceiver, pink and grizzly, 4"-5" long; and a Rainfish.

How to Hook a Bluefish. Bluefish strike hard and hook themselves most of the time. Nevertheless, set hard and if you miss, reel in fast, stop, and jig.

Other Fish Caught While Fishing for Bluefish. Jack crevalle, barracuda, Spanish mackerel, redfish, and snook.

Regulations

- Closed Season: none
- Minimum Size: 12" from tip of snout to fork in tail
- Maximum Size: no regulation
- Daily Bag Limit: 10

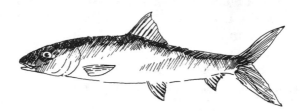

5

Bonefish; Banana Fish; Phantom; Silver Ghost; Ladyfish; Grubber
(Albula vulpes)

This highly sought-after fish is extremely strong; it can strip off 100 yd of line, make a right angle without stopping, and strip off another hundred yards—all in a few seconds. Although some people eat them, because of their many small bones, the bonefish is nearly always released. Preferred water temperature: 72°-80° F. All-tackle record: 19 lb.

WHERE AND WHEN

From Biscayne Bay down the Florida Keys to the Marquesas Keys beyond Key West, bonefish are typically a fish of the flats. The shallows near shore at low tide might be dry but during high water become feeding grounds for many varieties of fish. Although bonefish are occasionally caught far north of this region, no one intentionally fishes for them anywhere else in Florida. In this long island chain most bonefish are caught from Biscayne Bay to Islamorada Key. Oddly, even though bones are caught in the Marquesas, fishing for them is only fair between Marathon and Key West. Although bonefish are present all year in places such as Biscayne Bay, they are very sensitive to the water temperature and are usually numerous on the flats in the spring and early summer with April and May probably the best months and then again in October. During March they are getting ready to spawn and, if the water is warm enough, the largest fish can be caught then. When the water really heats up in August, bones can be found in the deeper water around the flats. In the winter afternoons, a grassy bottom will have warmed up enough to be comfortable for the fish. In the middle of summer when the sun bears down on the flats, a sand bottom reflects the light and the water remains relatively cool, as when it is overcast.

As with most saltwater fishes, early and late in the day and during spring tides are generally the best times to fish. Moving tidal water on the flats is a necessary condition, but the exact tidal stage to fish any given flat comes with observation and experience; some produce fish during the first part of the flood tide while others are better midway through a falling tide. When there is little or no water on the flats, bonefish frequently can be caught in the deeper channel edges or holes in the flats. A little breeze and a slight chop to the water will make bonefish less wary than a dead calm day. If the wind is blowing hard from the south or southeast, fish the ocean side flats; if it is from the north or northeast, try the Gulf side. Polaroid sunglasses in either yellow or amber are as necessary as a fishing rod.

TACKLE

Spinning and Plug Casting. A 6½'-8' rod that will cast a 1/8 oz bait; a reel holding at least 200 yd of 6#-10# line, mono; spin or conventional reel. (Note: Spinning tackle is easier to use with very light baits.)

Fly. A rod 8½'-9½' 7-10 weight. (Note: This is a *real* science!) Use a 7 weight rod when it is calm or when using small flies; an 8 weight rod with #4 and #2 flies; and a 9 or 10 weight rod when it is windy and/or when using epoxy lures; floating, sink-tip, a Bonefish Taper, or Monocore weight-forward line that is colored gray or at least not bright; a reel with a reliable drag system that will hold 200 yd of 12#-20# Micron or Dacron backing.

TECHNIQUES

Spinning and Plug Casting

Natural Bait

Live shrimp: This is the most reliable bonefish bait of all and not very long ago was the only bait used. Tie a bronze 1/0 or 2/0 hook directly to the line which should be doubled with a Bimini Twist. Or with a double surgeon's or Albright Special attach a short leader of 12# mono not over 1′ or so long. On very calm days when the water is clear, the fish flush easily so no leader is used. When it is a bit windy or the water is a little dirty, you can get away with a light leader.

Remove the tail fins of a lively shrimp and hook it one of several ways. 1) Under the chin and out the top of the head; 2) through the collar; or 3) remove the tail section and thread a hook up through the body and bring the point out either in the belly, side, or back (barbs in the shank of the hook help keep this kind of rigged shrimp in place). If you are using very light line—6# or less—casting a shrimp is easy. But if you need more weight when using heavier line or when it is windy, add a split shot or two to the line just ahead of the shrimp. A better way of doing this is the Texas rig.

Fishing with shrimp can be approached with or without chum. To chum one usually anchors a boat upcurrent and, if possible, with the sun and wind behind. Pick a sandy-grassy area known to host bonefish on a rising tide. Dice fresh shrimp into small pieces and scatter them in the chosen area. Crushed crab and cut-up conch can also be used. When you see bonefish feeding on the shrimp pieces, cast your shrimp about 6′-8′ beyond and in front of a fish; lift the rod tip just as the bait lands on the water and retrieve it so that it skips across the surface, then stop. Or you can just cast and leave your shrimp on the bottom, and wait for a bone to get its nose on your bait. Fishing without chum means wading the flats or casting from a flats boat, a shallow-draft skiff made especially for this type of water. Because bonefish are so sensitive to noise, a flats boat must be poled to within casting distance of a sighted fish. Wading offers an advantage as you can quickly follow a hooked fish to untangle the line from around a mangrove or sea fan. However, there are dangers in wading: an unknown flat may have deep holes, so scout it out during low tide; and, while wading, shuffle your feet along the sand bottom so as not to step on a sting ray.

From a boat or while wading, when a fish is sighted, if it is "mudding" or "tailing," you can safely cast to it as close as a foot or two. If it is cruising, cast no closer than 6' to it. A bait should land no closer than 10' in front of a school of bonefish. Follow the same instructions when casting to chummed-up fish. But when a bonefish picks up your bait no matter what style you are fishing, wait until the line becomes taut and then raise the rod tip and give it a short and easy set or two— nothing violent. As the fish takes off in its first powerful run, hold the rod tip high to keep the line out of water to avoid obstacles. That is why a long rod offers an advantage. Also, as the fish runs, do not touch the drag which should have been set to about ¼ of the strength of the line. When much line is out, loosen—don't tighten—the drag even more and don't reset to the original setting until you collect most of the line back on the reel.

Live crabs: Small blue crabs collected at low tide on the flats and ghost crabs collected on a beach at night or early in the morning are baits that catch bonefish, but they are not as effective as shrimp. Find a crab about the size of a quarter or a half dollar, break off the claws, and, using the same rig as described for shrimp, hook it from the bottom shell out through the top at the edge where the shell comes to a point. Re-hone the hook now because it must be extremely sharp. See the directions for fishing for permit with a crab, p. 70-71.

Artificial Bait. Used with or without a short leader of 12#-20#, one of the best lures is a small flatheaded skimmer jig from 1/8 oz-¼ oz in brown, tan, pink, or white. Tip it with a fingernail-sized piece of fresh shrimp and cast 15'-20' from a sighted fish. Retrieve with short flicks of the rod tip, the objective being to send up small puffs of sand to attract the bones. Use a Popeye made by Nickelure or a Gaines Wiggle Jig for tailing fish in shallow water and a Hampson-type for deeper water fish. Another good artificial is a 3"-4" Burke root beer colored worm to which weight is added by a couple of split shot or a Texas rig.

Cast ahead of the bonefish and retrieve slowly so that the lure works along the bottom. When you feel resistance, continue to retrieve and lift the rod tip at the same time to set the hook. On the flats, cast side-arm style instead of overhead and crouch to prevent spooking the fish. As already discussed, under fishing with shrimp, one can wade or fish from a flats skiff.

Fly Fishing

These days fly casting for bonefish is considered the ultimate fly fishing experience. When you think that a 9- or 10-pound fish in a few seconds can strip 200 yd of line from a tiny wand you are waving in the air, you'll have to agree this is special kind of sport. Fish from a flats boat or wade. On a calm day on shallow flats use a leader 12'-16' so as not to flush bonefish which always seem nervous. If there are obstructions such as mangroves that can tangle a line, use a 10# tippet; if there are none and the water is open, use a 6# tippet. As the wind picks up and/or the water deepens, the leader can be shortened to as little as 6'. Flies should be #8-#2, the smallest sizes being for calm, shallow flats. Weedless type flies are preferred and a few should be lightly weighted with lead wrapped around the hook shank. Floating line is basic; however, on deeper flats or when there is floating weed, a sinking line is better. Cast a foot in front of a tailing or mudding bonefish and retrieve the fly across its patch (never towards it) with strips of 1"-2", pausing occasionally. Keep the rod tip down in the water and speed up the retrieve if a fish comes after the fly. You can't get this close to a cruising fish or you will flush it; on windy days, however, you can get within a foot or two of any bonefish without scaring it away. With a weighted fly over sand, you should cast 20' or more in front of a school of bonefish and just leave the fly on the bottom. Whatever you do, don't cast so that line ends up over any fish in a school because they will immediately flush. When the fish are over the fly, retrieve so that it puffs up some sand. If a light-colored fly doesn't work, switch to a dark one—a big change like this is usually necessary to discover what works on any particular day. Chumming fish with shrimp, as described above, is also effective. When bonefish come to the scent, cast to them with a fly that has some color to it such as a Bonefish Special. Of the many flies available for bonefishing, the following are endorsed by most of the experts: Crazy Charley, Bonefish Special, Mother of Epoxy (MOE), a snapping shrimp imitation, Horror Fly, and the Frankie-Bell Bonefish Fly. Chocolate, white, tan, and pink are some of the colors to have in your fly box.

How to Release a Bonefish. There is no point in killing a bonefish as they are not much good to eat and a picture or two of what is now just dead meat is a high price to pay for a fish you could have caught again. When you have unhooked the fish, hold its tail and work it back and forth in the water; when it begins to struggle, release it by giving it a gentle shove in the direction of freedom.

Other Fish Caught While Bonefishing. Permit and occasionally barracuda.

Regulations

- Closed Season: none
- Minimum Size: 18″ overall
- Maximum Size: no regulation
- Daily Bag Limit: 1

6

Cobia; Ling; Lemonfish; Black Salmon; Runner; Black Kingfish; Crab-eater; Sergeantfish; Cabio

(Rachycentron canadum)

A hard-fighting fish that can strip a reel in a few seconds, cobia are a favorite sport fish primarily because they are plentiful and not difficult to catch. They are excellent to eat. Preferred water temperature: 68°-86° F. All-tackle record: 135 lb 9 oz.

WHERE AND WHEN

1. Atlantic coast, especially Key West Harbor where cobia are nearly always present from December to April. Wrecks near Key West, especially on the Gulf side, are known for cobia which frequently may be found as early as November and peak in February. In late March and April, cobia begin migrating north and they can usually be found off the lower and central coast from the shore out to beyond 100'; they are off Daytona Beach in early April, off Matanzas Inlet in late April, off the mouth of the St. Johns River in early May, and off Fernandina Inlet in late May and early June. Throughout their range, cobia lurk wherever buoys and navigation markers in at least 5' of water are present, whether close in to shore or farther offshore. They bite best when there is current, but they are also caught during the tidal stand.

2. Gulf coast, especially in the Panhandle in late February and March. Cobia are then found down the entire coast as the run gets going in mid-April and peaks from June through August at which time the largest fish of the year are caught. Throughout their range, cobia can be found on the sand bar between inner and outer sloughs and a few miles out near markers and buoys.

TACKLE

Spinning and Plug Casting. About a 7′ rod for moderate casting; 12#-20# line, mono or braided; spin or conventional reel.

Surf and Pier. A 9′-11′ rod with 20#-30# line, mono or braided; spin or conventional reel that holds at least 200 yd of line.

Fly. 8½′-9½′ 8-10 weight rod and line; weight-forward, floating line with at least 200 yd of 20# Dacron backing.

TECHNIQUES

Live Bait. Migrating cobia can be spotted as they travel in shallow water or hang around pilings, navigation markers, and buoys. Very often they stick close to sharks and rays and if one of these is sighted, it pays to run the boat nearby, approaching from behind the animal. However, many cobia are caught from fishing piers and from the beach during their migration so a boat isn't absolutely essential. Live bait is the cobia's downfall and the noisier, the better. Grunts, because of the sound they are named for, are excellent, but pinfish, blue runners, or nearly any other small fish will produce. In the northeast, menhaden are trolled slowly and eels, if available, are considered attractive bait. For the highly rated fishing in Key West Harbor, catfish with spines removed are considered the best bait. Large live shrimp and small blue crabs also are good.

If pier or surf fishing, pass a 2 oz-4 oz egg sinker on the line (or use a fish finder rig), attach a swivel, and tie on about 3′ of 30#-50# mono for a leader. Hook the bait in front of the dorsal fin with a 4/0-7/0 O'Shaughnessy. If fishing near pilings or markers, omit the lead unless a strong current compels you to use an ounce or two. If wreck fishing you may need still more weight. If fishing over shallow reefs, attach a float about 4' above the bait. When fishing markers or buoys, keep the boat 40'-50' away and cast. Chumming up cobia from markers or wrecks is usually successful. When choosing a marker or buoy or any piece of structure you can see, fish one that has a good growth of barnacles and oysters and also is in a part of a channel less used by boats. Mid-day fishing from a boat is often productive as at this time fish are more easily spotted—and remember to use Polaroid sunglasses.

Artificial Bait. Because casting to a sighted fish with an artificial is easier and more accurate than throwing a live bait, this method is not only popular but is productive, as well. Lures should be cast across the path of a moving cobia, whether it is traveling with a ray or swimming near a marker. When the lure is near the fish, give it plenty of action. Also, one should cast near a hooked cobia as several of his buddies often tag along. Artificials that have been successful are a bucktail jig (adding a strip of squid will help) in white, lime-green, yellow, and chartreuse, 3/4 oz-1 oz; multi-colored jigs such as Pete's Ling Jig and No Alibi Jigs found in the Panhandle; any noisy sinking and diving plug in silver, white, chartreuse, or light blue; tube lures; and a 12" black plastic worm, Texas-rigged. For deep jigging around wrecks, try heavy bucktail jigs to 4 oz with a plastic worm added and the same size diamond jigs and touts. Frequently, cobia hit a jig as it descends so be ready; this means raising and lowering the rod tip is a better technique than bouncing a jig off the bottom. When a cobia strikes an artificial, delay striking for a split second.

Fly. The best way to fish cobia with a fly rod is to bring the fish within casting distance with chum or by catching one on live bait and bringing it and its traveling companions close-by. Use a loud, large popper or a 7" white Deceiver tied with some mylar.

What To Do If a Hooked Cobia Heads for a Marker. You will probably be unable to stop a cobia headed for a marker or buoy without breaking the fishing line. If you can't turn the fish, free spool with your thumb lightly on the spool to prevent a backlash, and let the fish run. Go up to the marker to free the line and then throw the reel in gear to begin the fight again.

How to Land a Cobia. With probably the worst reputation as a tough fish to boat, cobia must be dealt with carefully. Not only do they often explode at boatside, but even though you might think the fish is whipped and you are able to sink in the gaff, it might still be "green" and so begin a characteristic twisting and rolling action that for many fishermen has meant a loss of fish and equipment. For one thing, the gaff should have a loop of ¼" line attached through a hole in the shaft a few inches below the grip. Secure it around your wrist and gaff the fish by reaching across its back (being careful not to touch it) with the point down. Bring it back towards you, the object being to stick the gaff under the backbone. If the fish is truly tired, all this will work; but if it is still "green," you've got to hold on until it is exhausted. Try to swing the fish from the water into the fish box in one motion and then sit on the lid; a "green" cobia on the cockpit floor can destroy most anything in its path.

Other Fish Caught While Fishing for Cobia. Kingfish, amberjack, tripletail, permit, and grouper.

Regulations

- Closed Season: none
- Minimum Size: 33" from nose to fork of tail
- Maximum Size: no regulation
- Daily Bag Limit: 2
- Note: Cobia must be landed and brought in with head and fins intact.

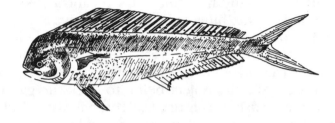

7

Dolphin; Mahi-Mahi; Dorado

(Coryphaena hippurus)

A strong, highly colorful, jumping fish that is among the world's greatest on light tackle. Most often in schools of a few fish to a few dozen, the largest dolphin are found as pairs or singles. They taste great. Preferred water temperature: 78°-85° F. All-tackle record: 87 lb.

WHERE AND WHEN

1. A Gulf Stream fish primarily, so all along the Atlantic coast in blue water, especially from Palm Beach south with the Keys being the best area. Some fish, however, do stray shoreward and can be found in green water, a few sometimes even off fishing piers. Farther south, the fishing is year-round while in the northern part of the state, only the summer. Generally April to August is prime time in the Keys and most of South Florida on the Atlantic side. In July and August one may have to fish 20-30 miles offshore. Off

Daytona Beach, St. Augustine, and Jacksonville, dolphin are often 50 or more miles out in the ocean.

2. Gulf coast dolphin fishing is available but isn't nearly as attractive as the opposite coast. In the summer off the southwest coast, sometimes as much as 40-60 miles at sea, dolphin up to 5 or 10 lb are caught. In the last few years, however, Gulf of Mexico currents have been changing and seem to be improving dolphin fishing.

TACKLE

Spinning and Plug Casting. A 7' rod; 8#-15# line, mono or braided; spin or conventional reel.

Trolling. A 20#-30# outfit, mono or braided line; a stand-up rod about 5½' with about 7 guides; spin or conventional reel.

Fly. A 7 weight 8½'-9' rod with line to match; floating or intermediate sinking line, weight-forward; on windy days, up to a 9 weight outfit; a reel holding 200 yd of 20#-30# backing, either Micron or Dacron.

TECHNIQUES

Ocean Trolling

Natural Bait. Use a 3'-6' 40#-50# mono leader or #7 tobacco-stained stainless steel, a medium-size ballyhoo, strip, or whole mullet and a 7/0 hook. Troll from the outrigger or flat lines at a speed to make the bait alternately swim and skip over the water. Fish near weed lines and color changes, under circling man-o-war birds, and run by any floating object such as a log, a box, a large clump of weed, etc. as dolphin often are in the shade. Sometimes, if fish are difficult to find, trolling a large teaser helps (see the blue marlin chapter on using "bird" teasers, p. 62). If there's a school, just a chunk of ballyhoo or mullet on a hook will work. To keep the school nearby, leave a hooked fish in the water until another is hooked; then bring in the first but leave the second in the water until still another is hooked. Or you can tie a 6' piece of mono leader to a plastic jug, tie on a hook and bait with a chunk of fish and leave it in the water even after a fish is hooked. Follow the jug and you'll always be with the school. Although you can switch to artificial bait when in a school of dolphin, occasionally throw a handful of cut-up bait to keep the fish nearby. A plastic skirt, a feather jig, or a Sea Witch around the head of a trolled ballyhoo or mullet is a good idea and yellow seems to be the best color. Beneath the small schooling fish (called "chickens" if they are 6 or 7 lb, "peanuts" if smaller) are often large dolphin. Hook a small live bait fish such as a 12" mullet or a blue runner through the lips and troll slowly near the school and you'll have a chance at not only a "bull" dolphin (a male; females are called "cows") but a blue marlin, as well. In addition, once dolphin grow to 15 or 20 lb and travel singly or in pairs, look for them a hundred yards or more from the weed lines. Fish for these larger dolphin as described above.

Artificial Bait. More ocean can be covered with artificials because your boat can travel up to 10 or 12 mph and this is no problem to a fish that can swim over 40 mph. Yellow or yellow and green Japanese feathers up to 6" long are standard trolling lures and a Moldcraft Softhead "bird" trolled in front of the feather often helps. A red and white feather over a ballyhoo trolled far behind the boat is considered a good tactic for large fish. Other lures are the No Alibi, the artificial strip bait, and the Dolphin Jr. with a plastic tail or pork rind trailing behind. Deep plugs such as the Rebel, Magnum Rapala, and others trolled from a flat line or downrigger are effective. If fish are in a feeding frenzy, even a white rag on a hook will catch fish.

Casting

Spin and Plug. Using a Bimini Twist, double the fishing line into a loop at least as long as the rod and with a swivel attach a 1' 40# mono leader; you can by-pass the swivel by tying the line to the leader with a double surgeon's knot. Cruise in the boat (or troll until fish are found) and when floating material such as previously mentioned is sighted or when you see birds diving and/or fish breaking the water's surface, get ready. Approach quietly and cast nearby, working the lure quickly. If the fish tire of one kind of artificial, switch to another. Use a white or yellow bucktail or nylon jig, about a 3/8 oz-3/4 oz; a Zara-type plug; and a Burke Flex-O-Plug. Because dolphin are really wild in the cockpit or fish box and dangerous with several treble hooks to remove, replace the treble hooks with single hooks, about 4/0-6/0.

Fly. Use a 7′ leader with a 15# tippet. Cast to a sighted fish and after twitching the fly two or three times, allow it to sink motionlessly. Or, if this doesn't work, retrieve by stripping rapidly. Sometimes one need only lower a fly over the side of a boat to hook up in a school of dolphin. Use a sinking line if the water is choppy or to get below the smaller fish to where the bigger ones wait. Use a 3/0-6/0 Seaducer in red and yellow; any yellow streamer; a white popping bug up to a 3/0; and a glass minnow imitation.

How to Hook a Dolphin. These hard-striking fish will often hook themselves but a hard set or two is in order at all times.

Other Fish Caught While Fishing for Dolphin. Sailfish, white marlin, blue marlin, tunas, and wahoo.

Regulations

- Closed Season: none
- Minimum Size: no regulation
- Maximum Size: no regulation
- Daily Bag Limit: 10

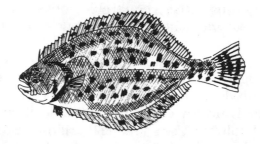

8

Flounders

Not only are flounders or flatfishes delicious to eat, but they put up a strong, hard-pulling battle. There are many kinds of flounder, but for the angler in Florida the International Game Fish Association (IGFA) keeps records on the following:

- Summer flounder (*Paralichthys dentatus*), 22 lb 7 oz, found only in northeast Florida during the spring and summer.
- Southern or mud flounder (*Paralichthys lethostigma*), 20 lb 9 oz, found in all parts of Florida except in the south and is caught mainly in cold weather in water varying from salty to fresh.

The IGFA keeps no records on another Florida flounder, the Gulf or sand flounder (*Paralichthys albigutta*) which grows to about 15″ and although it can be found in all parts of Florida during the spring and summer, is not common. The information that follows refers primarily to the Southern flounder but applies to others, as well. This species puts up with water temperatures from 50°-90° F.

WHERE AND WHEN

1. Atlantic coast, especially Matanzas Inlet beginning in October and Sebastian Inlet on very cold days beginning

with the first cold front in December. These migrating fish spend the winter in Florida and although the big "door-mats" are generally inlet fish, smaller ones are caught in inside water.

2. Gulf coast, especially in shallow bays, estuaries, and passes in the Panhandle beginning in November and in deep passes and along rock jetties in the summer.

TACKLE

Spinning and Plug Casting. A 5'-7' rod for medium to heavy use; 15#-30# line, mono or braided; spin or conventional reel.

Bottom. A 6'-9' rod for medium to heavy use; 20#-40# line, mono or braided; spin or conventional reel.

TECHNIQUES

Natural Bait

Mullet: Along the Atlantic coast, live finger mullet are by far the best bait. After buying or netting them some effort must be given to transporting and keeping them alive. Keep them in a large plastic garbage can with an efficient pump for air. To rig a mullet, use a sliding sinker rig with a ½-2 oz egg sinker (heavy enough to keep the bait on the bottom) above a black barrel swivel. Attach 1' of 40#-50# mono and use a #4 or #6 treble hook or a single short shank 1/0 or 2/0 hook. Hook mullet through the upper lip, behind the dorsal fin, or behind the anal fin. Fish in deep water at the edge of an inlet near rocks. Flounder can be found anywhere in this area and the whole length of the jetty—both sides, from inside to the mouth and around to the ocean side—should be fished. Carefully fish bridge pilings as well; flounder like protected water downtide of such structure because it shields them from the current and gives them a vantage point to attack bait passing by. Any tide except slack is alright with most of the action occurring during the high parts of the ebb and flood. Dirty water makes for poor flounder fishing.

Bull minnow: In the Panhandle these are considered the best bait; they can be bought in bait and tackle stores or caught.

Hook them through the lips and fish from a boat, drifting in passes along rock jetties, mud ledges, and sand bars until fish are found. Anchor and cast out a bull minnow and reel in a few feet of line every minute or so. Pier fishing is also good for Panhandle flounder; try to get the same bull minnow bait under the pier and work it out into the open slowly.

Shrimp: Large shrimp do catch flounder but they are definitely second-best to bait fish. Hook one through the horn on its head or thread it on the hook. Use the same rig as for mullet and fish the same way.

Artificial Bait. A few fish are caught with artificials but it is not a very productive way to fish for flounder. But around the barges in Tampa Bay and the middle and upper Atlantic inlets fishermen have been successful using jigs. Fish one right on the bottom near pilings or rocks and weight it, if necessary, with a ¼-½ oz egg sinker above the swivel. Use a light 2' leader, about 12#-15# mono. Retrieve very slowly. Try a yellow bucktail jig with or without a small bait fish (attached by hooking through the lips), a Cotee Glitter Shad, and small, deep-running plugs.

How to Hook a Flounder. The mistake most anglers make in flounder fishing is setting the hook too early. First you must distinguish the strike from current and bait action: the strike is just a tap or two or a thump. The fish should be allowed to swim off with the bait in its mouth while the fisherman free spools the line. Exactly when to set the hook is debatable: some fishermen do so after 15 seconds and others wait up to 2 minutes. With an artificial, a somewhat shorter wait is required.

How to Land a Flounder. Because a lot of heavy pulling will be going on, it takes stout tackle to keep the fish away from rocks or pilings. Therefore, light tackle is useful only when fishing from a boat in open water.

Other Fish Caught While Fishing for Flounder. Bluefish, snook, spotted seatrout, redfish, jack crevalle, and shark.

Regulations

- Closed Season: none
- Minimum Size: 12″ overall
- Maximum Size: no regulation
- Daily Bag Limit: 10

9

Groupers

Very powerful fishes that demand heavy tackle, groupers are bottom fishermen's favorites. The following are Florida species for which the International Game Fish Association keeps all-tackle records:

- Black grouper (*Mycteroperca bonaci*) 114 lb, found all around Florida in water over 60' deep.
- Gag or gray grouper (*Mycteroperca microlepis*) 80 lb 6 oz, found all around Florida in water over 60' deep.
- Yellowfin grouper (*Mycteroperca venenosa*) 40 lb 12 oz, found in south Florida in offshore water.
- Scamp (*Mycteroperca phenax*) 29 lb, found all around Florida in water 75'-300' deep.
- Red Hind (*Epinephelus guttatus*) 6 lb 1 oz, found all around Florida except the northern Gulf coast in water 80'-350' deep.
- Nassau grouper (*Epinephelus striatus*) 38 lb 8 oz, found all around Florida in relatively shallow water under 100' deep.
- Red grouper (*Epinephelus morio*) 42 lb 4 oz, found all around Florida in water from 80'-400' deep.
- Warsaw grouper (*Epinephelus nigritus*) 436 lb 12 oz, found all around Florida usually in very deep water over 350'.
- Jewfish (*Epinephelus itajara*) 680 lb, found all around Florida in relatively shallow water under 100' deep.

WHERE AND WHEN

Groupers are caught all year, all over the state from shallow water inside passes and bays to offshore. On the Gulf coast they may be found up to 60 miles out. The one basic fact of grouper life that unifies them is that they all prefer some sort of bottom structure and are nearly always found around pilings, rocks, wrecks, reefs, etc. Every fishing locality has its special grouper holes but some are, of course, secret and probably will never be known to any except a few local fishermen. However, many of the best wrecks, holes, reefs, dropoffs, and ledges are free for the finding; other excellent ones are in published lists of such locations and can be bought in bait and tackle stores. The desired information is in the form of land and marker bearings, latitude and longitude, or, the best of all, Loran coordinates. This compels the boater to install this device but Loran has become very necessary for the serious bottom fisherman. Here are some places and times grouper are caught on the Gulf coast: gag come close inshore in September in Southwest Florida and may be found along with black grouper from November through March in 25′-45′ of water, about 15-30 miles or so offshore (but in the summer 40-60 miles out), and Tampa Bay in November around the shipping channels. Find red grouper in August in 60′-70′ of water in the passes in the southwest in the fall on a slack tide and farther north off Apalachee Bay in the summer around 50′ and in the winter around 15′. Along the northeast coast grouper begin biting in mid-May. The Keys during the winter in 30′-100′ of water, the deep wrecks in over 300′ on the Atlantic side of Key West, and in 80′-120′ of water over the reefs in February and in June when black grouper move in to spawn are also productive. Fish the Panhandle during the winter from a couple of miles from shore to 20 miles out (if the weather allows you to make it). One may fish the southeast during the spring but the largest grouper are taken in January and February. Although it is evident that grouper generally move inshore during cold weather and do the opposite in warm, the jewfish is the exception: July in relatively shallow water is the best time and place to find these immense fish. Look for them in backwater areas such as holes around mangrove islands, docks, and undercut banks along which there is current. Nighttime is best and 12/0 forged steel hooks plus a light chain leader are often used.

TACKLE

Trolling. A stand-up rod about 5½'; 30#-50# line, mono, braided, Dacron, or wire; conventional reel, about a 4/0.

Bottom Fishing. A heavy glass rod, preferably a 5½' stand-up type; 50# line, mono or braided Dacron; a conventional 4/0 reel.

Deep Water (200' or more) Bottom Fishing. A solid glass rod between 7' and 8'; 100# mono or Dacron line; 6/0 conventional or electric reel.

TECHNIQUES

Trolling. Used as a method in itself or just to locate grouper, trolling has the advantage of enabling the angler to cover a lot of territory in a short amount of time. Keys' patch reefs, acres of dark grass and other water life amid white sand in 8'-20' of water, are well known for top small grouper fishing and are especially productive after a cold front has moved through and the water is clear. Trolling patch reefs uncovers fish sooner than bottom fishing in one spot will. Because grouper run heavy and pull hard, it is necessary to turn a fish away from its place in the bottom structure. For this reason a 50# outfit is the safe way to fish. Attach to the end of the line a large — even marlin-size — ball bearing black swivel and to this tie on 4' of 60#-80# mono as a leader. On the business end of this you can use the following: a rigged ballyhoo with a Japanese feather ahead of it; a good deep-running plug such as the Magnum Rapala, Mann's Stretch 25+, the Rebel Jawbreaker, a saltwater Rat-L-Trap, the Boone Cairns Swimmer (any plug can be used if you place a trolling lead from ½ to 1 lb ahead of it, but you need a very long leader to separate the plug from the weight and this complicates landing a fish); a spoon such as the Acetta 2180 blue or red on wire line, a planer, or a downrigger; or a slow-trolled live bait. Plugs should have a light-colored or silver bottom and backs of blue, blue and yellow, black, or mackerel finish. Many fishermen remove the treble hooks that come with large plugs and replace them with Mustad stainless steel double hooks on the front and rear of the plug, leaving no hook in the middle spot. Attach the plug to the leader with either a marlin-size snap swivel or a large loop in the mono so it can move freely. Troll plugs up to 100' behind the boat and don't be afraid to move right along; 7 or 8 knots is not too fast. To change a plug's course through the water, bend its eye in the direction you wish it to travel.

Other commonly caught groupers for which the IGFA keeps no records are Graysby (*Epinephelus cruentatus*) and the Yellowmouth grouper (*Mycteroperca interstitialis*).

All of these groupers succumb to the same general fishing techniques. Most are good to eat but all, especially when large, may cause ciguatera, or fish poisoning—a very dangerous illness. All groupers are warm water fishes that are numerous when the water is in the upper seventies, at least. The jewfish likes water temperature in the eighties.

Bottom Fishing

Passes: Especially from Boca Grande south through the Everglades National Park area, shallow water pass fishing for smaller grouper is very productive. Chum with heads and shells of shrimp as well as small cut pieces and use the whole shrimp as bait. A 2' leader of 50# mono and a 2/0 short shank strong hook are necessary. In addition to shrimp, other bait such as crabs and small live fish will work.

Open water: There are nearly as many ways to bottom-fish in deep water as there are fishermen. Once fish are found, the objective is to lower to them a natural looking morsel. This is easier said than done as the heavy lead which is necessary to carry the bait swiftly to the bottom interferes with its natural action in the water. To combat this, the fish finder rig is used with a sliding egg sinker, the size depending on the depth. Add about 3' of 100#-125# mono leader and a Mustad 3407 hook to match the size of fish hunted—4/0-7/0 will handle most situations. As you go very deep, particularly where there is a strong current, 1 lb of lead is not too much. The guppy rig may be preferable since with each added hook you get an additional chance; also, because the sinker hits a rocky bottom before the hooks reach it, you can stop the descent and avoid losing a rig. For very deep fishing, when so much line is out that you cannot feel the action and therefore may miss the strike, the Japanese circle hook has the advantage of hooking the fish without your having to set up. Chumming is the key to successful grouper fishing of this type, and any kind of ground-up fish mixed with bread or some other kind of extender will attract fish.

Canned fish, such as tuna or cat food, works well, too. You must anchor the boat upcurrent of the chosen spot so that the chum and baits will drift down to the fish. Live bait usually catches the largest grouper and is especially good when drifting and not using chum; try small jack crevalle, blue runners (hard tails), ballyhoo, pinfish, porgies, menhaden, small snapper, grunts, and hook one through the top lip. But dead cut bait works well enough in a chum line and is certainly more convenient. Each locality has its favorite cut bait but some species have found favor everywhere: mullet, Spanish sardines, cigar minnows, bonito, squirrel fish, salted ladyfish (skipjack), and squid. The proper technique in any bottom fishing is to slowly lower the baited rig so that the leader doesn't wrap around the fishing line. This may happen anyway, so when the lead hits the bottom, crank up a few feet and forcefully raise the rod tip high over your head and then slowly lower it to the water's surface. Do this several times and the leader will clear itself from the line. If you are using a fish finder rig, let the lead rest on the bottom and keep the reel in free spool so that an interested fish can easily pull line away. If you are using a guppy rig or anything similar, when the lead touches bottom, raise it a foot or two and fish from this position.

When a grouper bites, let it take the bait until you feel a hard, continuous pull; this may take five minutes or more. Then, with the reel drag set so tight it is difficult to pull line off it, set the hook and reel in the line quickly; the objective is to turn the fish's head immediately to prevent it from going into its hole in the rocks or reef.

Jigging. If grouper have been located, working a jig over them not only catches fish but saves bait. Chumming helps, but it is not always necessary. Depending on the depth, jigs up to 8 oz can be used. (A fair guideline to follow regarding how much weight to use for a given depth is as follows: 1 oz for 25'; 2 oz for up to 50'; and 3 oz for about 100'.) The standard is a white or yellow bean-shaped jig which is best fished with something added to it. A strip of fish belly, a squid strip, a plastic worm, or the Cotee Tip-it will improve the chances of catching fish. A dead ballyhoo can be used in a couple of ways. Attach two 5/0 hooks with wire to the eye of a 1-2 oz jig, break off the bill of a ballyhoo, and pass the jig's hook through its lips. Stick the two added hooks into the bait's belly.

Or you can butterfly a ballyhoo to make a fine jigging bait. Fillet it along the back but let the two formed sides remain attached at the front end. Remove the head and backbone and hook the ballyhoo through both halves in the front end with a 6/0 hook; then add an ounce or two of lead to get it down in the water. Regardless of the jig used, lower it and when it hits bottom you will immediately recognize it because the line suddenly becomes slack. Then, sharply raise the rod tip and just as quickly lower it to water level. How much of an arc the rod tip makes going through the air as you raise it depends on the fisherman coaching you. The best solution is to raise it over your head and all points in-between; that is, vary the jigging until you discover what is working that day. Continue with this all the while varying the speed and distance you make the jig hop off the bottom until you find the right combination. If you are drifting, as line goes out there will come a time when you can't feel the jig very accurately. When this happens, it is not on the bottom at all. The stronger the current, the sooner this happens, so be alert to it and reel in and start over again. As with bottom fishing with bait, keep the reel's drag set tight to prevent a fish from going into its hole.

How to Land a Grouper. It is not uncommon for a grouper, if given its head, to hole-up for a while in the bottom structure it calls home, and it is very difficult to avoid breaking the line attempting to pull it back out. There are two methods to solve this problem. One is to keep as taut a line as possible and wait for the fish to come out. The other way is to let the line go slack for up to fifteen minutes and then reel in suddenly and quickly; if the fish comes out either way, continue pressuring it on its way to the surface.

Other Fish Caught While Fishing for Grouper. Amberjack, kingfish, snapper, African pompano, and an occasional sailfish when using live bait on an outer reef off the southeast coast and the Keys.

Regulations

- Closed Season: none
- Minimum Size: 20″ overall
- Maximum Size: no regulation
- Daily Bag Limit: 5 (single species or mixed)
- Note: Groupers must be brought in with head and fins intact.
- Note: The minimum size does not apply to the graysby or red hind. Each boat may have, in addition to the bag limit of 5, one extra speckled hind and one extra Warsaw grouper. There is a closed season on all jewfish and Nassau grouper.

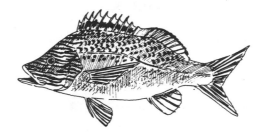

10

Grunts

These small, shallow water fishes are caught by anyone fishing for snapper. They are very numerous, are great fun for children to catch, make good live bait for large fishes, and are fair for eating. The International Game Fish Association keeps records on the following grunts:

- Margate (*Haemulon album*) 15 lb 12 oz, found along the Atlantic coast of Florida.
- White grunt (*Haemulon plumieri*) 6 lb 8 oz, found primarily along the Atlantic coast of Florida.

The common Florida grunts that the IGFA does not keep records for are the tomtate (*Haemulon aurolineatum*) which reaches 10"; the Spanish or gray grunt (*Haemulon macrostomum*) which reaches 17"; the cottonwick (*Haemulon melanurum*) which reaches 13"; the sailor's choice (*Haemulon parrai*) which reaches about 1'; the bluestriped grunt (*Haemulon sciurus*) which reaches about 1'; the striped grunt (*Haemulon striatum*) which reaches about 1'; the pigfish (*Orthopristis chrysoptera*) which reaches 15"; and the porkfish (*Anisotremus virginicus*) which reaches 15". Preferred water temperature: 66°-86° F.

WHERE AND WHEN

The same as for the reef-dwelling and shallow-water snappers, see p. 110.

TACKLE

The same as for small snappers, see p. 110.

TECHNIQUES

The same as for small snappers, see p. 111.

Other Fish Caught While Fishing for Grunts. Snappers, groupers, Spanish mackerel, and jack crevalle.

Regulations (none)

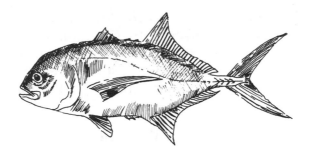

11

Jacks

The jack crevalle is the best known member of this group; it is a pugnacious and voracious fish that rushes small bait fishes up over a sea wall or chases them on to a beach. It is a most willing combatant and is exciting to catch on light tackle. Well-known relatives discussed elsewhere in this book are the amberjack, permit, and pompano. But there are other jacks that are worthy of being sought out; the International Game Fish Association keeps records on the following:

- Jack crevalle (*Caranx hippos*) 57 lb 5 oz, found all around Florida in inshore, inlet, and open ocean.
- Horse-eye jack (*Caranx latus*) 24 lb 8 oz, found all around Florida inshore and offshore, over reefs, and in deep holes and channels near flats.
- Yellow jack (*Caranx bartholomaei*) 19 lb 7 oz, found all around Florida but not very common.
- Blue runner (*Caranx crysos*) 8 lb 7 oz, found all around Florida in shallow water about 6′ deep over grassy areas off beaches and out to the reefs.
- Cottonmouth jack (*Uraspis secunda*) 4 lb 8 oz, found all around Florida.
- Rainbow runner (*Elagatis bipinnulata*) 37 lb 9 oz, found all around Florida in the open ocean.

• African pompano (*Alectis ciliaris*) 50 lb 8 oz, found all around Florida usually near rocks, reefs, and wrecks.

The IGFA does not keep records for the bar jack (*Caranx ruber*) and it grows to over 4 lb. The rainbow runner, blue runner, and bar jack are excellent for eating. Large jacks can cause ciguatera poisoning if eaten, a sometimes fatal disease in humans. Preferred water temperature: 70°-80° F. for most of the jacks above.

WHERE AND WHEN

1. Jack crevalle, the most wide-ranging and numerous of the group, can be found all over Florida in the surf, around and inside inlets, on the flats, in the Intracoastal Waterway and the canals connecting to it. Aggressive fish such as these often hunt in packs and trap bait fish against some land structure. Therefore, searching for them along seawalls, bridge pilings, inlet jetties, and in canals is highly rewarding, particularly during the winter when they seek inshore waters for warmth. From spring through fall they can be found in the ocean from shore to reef.
2. The bays along the Gulf coast and in the Panhandle such as Apalachicola and Choctawhatchee Bays are known to produce large jack crevalle in the spring and fall.
3. People rarely go fishing just for the other jacks; rather, they are caught when an angler is seeking something else.

TACKLE

Spinning and Bait Casting. For shallow-water fishing, light equipment such as a 5½'-6½' rod, preferably graphite; 4#-8# line, mono or braided; a reel holding 200 yd; or a heavier outfit such as 10#-15# and a slightly longer rod.

Fly. A 9 weight rod with a weight-forward, floating line to match; 400 yd of 20#-30# Micron or Dacron backing.

TECHNIQUES

Natural Bait. Jacks feed on swimming fish and any small fish hooked through the back, in front of the dorsal fin or in any other way will work—jacks are not particular. In Panhandle bays in August and September large jack crevalle in the forty-pound range are customarily caught on big, live menhaden which are hooked through the nose, behind the dorsal fin, or just ahead of the anal fin. These are freelined or fished with a float. Sight schools of fish or chum with live menhaden that have been stunned before release by throwing them hard on the boat deck or the water's surface. For live-baiting, use 2'-3' of 30#-40# mono as a leader and attach it directly to the line with a double surgeon's knot or to a swivel with an improved clinch knot.

Artificial Bait. Of all the fishes in the sea, jack crevalle are the most cooperative when it comes to fishing with artificials. Anything from a ¼ oz or larger fast-moving jig in white or yellow with or without a plastic tail, a noisy surface plug, an under-surface swimming plug, or a spoon will work; except for the largest and wisest jacks, it is unnecessary to use anything but artificials. Use a 20#-30# mono leader cut to a size that enables comfortable casting. When a jack comes up behind a lure, always speed it up and work the rod tip in hard jerks; they seem to love the chase and a slow-moving bait just doesn't excite them.

Fly. For these unsophisticated fish, the leader is not so critical. It can be around 6' with a 30# butt and a tippet of 8#-12# or lighter if you handle the fish delicately; large jacks surely deserve a 16# tippet. Fly selection is not too important: glass minnows, popping bugs, and a white Deceiver with Mylar tied into it will catch fish as will many other streamer-types. Just make certain that when a fish zeroes in on your fly, strip in rapidly.

Other Fish Caught While Fishing for Jacks. In shallow water: snook, bluefish, Spanish mackerel, spotted seatrout, and redfish—in deeper reef water: kingfish, sailfish, amberjack, and cero mackerel.

Regulations only for African pompano

- Closed season: none
- Minimum Size: 24" from tip of nose to fork of tail
- Maximum Size: no regulation
- Daily Bag Limit: 2 per day, person or vessel, whichever is less

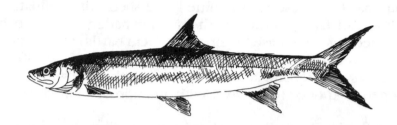

Ladyfish; Ten Pounder; Skipjack
(Elops saurus)

An extremely sporty fish on light tackle, the ladyfish may be one of the most overlooked fighting fishes in Florida. It puts on a jumping display, makes great cut bait for other fishes, and is plentiful. Ladyfish are very bony and are rarely eaten. All-tackle record: 5 lb 14 oz.

WHERE AND WHEN

1. Atlantic coast, especially in the south and in the Keys where they are caught all year.
2. Gulf coast, especially in the Everglades National Park area where they are caught all year. In the northern part of this coast, they leave for the winter but reappear in March or April and remain until it gets cold again.

TACKLE

Spinning and Plug Casting. A 6'-7' rod for very light use; 4#-8# line, mono or braided; spin or conventional reel.

Fly. A 5 weight rod if it isn't windy, a 7 weight if it is; weight-forward or shooting taper floating line; small fresh water trout reel.

TECHNIQUES

Inlet and Beach

Natural Bait. See the rigs recommended for pompano and blue-fish, p. 75 and 12, and use a shock tippet of 20#-30# mono; most any combination of hook and sinker will work. Use bait such as sand fleas and shrimp—alive or dead—and mullet, cut into strips. Fish the beach and inlet mouths in 6'-8' of water early in the morning and in late afternoon during a strong tidal flow. The last few hours of both the flood and ebb tides are best. Nighttime fishing is good. On the Gulf coast, frigate birds over shallow water sometimes mean ladyfish.

Artificial Bait. Use ¼ oz-⅜ oz white or yellow feather or nylon jigs, surface and just-beneath-the-surface plugs, and streamer flies that imitate small bait fish or poppers and sliders.

Flats

Natural Bait. Use the riggings and baits described earlier for inlet and beach fishing.

Artificial Bait. Find shallow, grassy flats, deeper basins in Florida Bay, mangrove shores, and the edges of channels. The presence of glass minnows is a good sign. Cast into likely spots and work from the bottom up in short jerks. Vary the retrieval speed until the correct one is found; this might change from day to day. Use ¼ oz-⅜ oz white or yellow feather or nylon jigs, surface and just-beneath-the-surface plugs, and streamer flies that imitate small bait fish or poppers and sliders.

How to Hook and Land a Ladyfish. The fish has a tender mouth so strong hook setting might tear the hook loose. Successfully land-ing a ladyfish means bowing to the fish when using very light tackle by immediately lowering the rod tip when the fish jumps.

An actively jumping fish such as this requires some care; one cannot horse it in.

Other Fish Caught While Fishing for Ladyfish. Spotted seatrout, snook, pompano, bluefish, and jack crevalle.

Regulations (none)

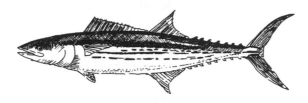

Cero Mackerel
(Scomberomorus regalis)

Very much like its close relative, the Spanish mackerel, cero are also good sport on light tackle. They are considered excellent for eating. Preferred water temperature: 70°-80° F. All-tackle record: 17 lb 2 oz.

WHERE AND WHEN

Southeast Florida, especially the Keys, in the fall and winter. Cero are generally sighted in schools feeding on ballyhoo over patch reefs in 18'-20' of water and over deeper reefs to 60'

TACKLE

The same as for Spanish mackerel, p. 55.

TECHNIQUES

Cero can be caught using tackle and methods listed for Spanish mackerel. One of the best ways is to chum over a reef until ballyhoo are attracted. Net or catch some of these to use live for the cero which will appear looking for ballyhoo. Freeline the live bait, use a float, or kite fish (see Sailfish section). A stinger hook is recommended. Fast trolling a Clark or Squid spoon is a good technique.

Other Fish Caught While Fishing for Cero Mackerel. Spanish mackerel, kingfish, and sailfish.

Regulations (none)

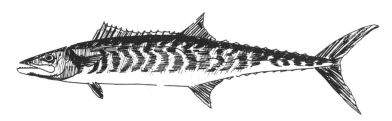

14

King Mackerel; Kingfish;
Giant Mackerel; King
(Scomberomorus cavalla)

A migratory, schooling fish that leaps out of water in a spectacular show, the kingfish has great power for short runs. It's very good to eat. Preferred water temperature: 70°-75° F. All-tackle record: 90 lb.

WHERE AND WHEN

Kingfish are caught in the reef area, from piers, and even in the surf along the entire coast of Florida—they have also been caught 50 miles or more offshore of North Florida along the Continental Shelf. The Keys, the mouth of Tampa Bay, and the lower southeast coast are well-known kingfishing locations, but this fish can be easily caught elsewhere. They show up in the southern part of the state in the fall—generally October—and remain until March or April and sometimes even into May. Off the northern part of the two coasts some kingfish action can be found in the fall but when the water cools, as in December, to below 67° or 68°, kingfish are absent; they return in the spring and summer. Early in the season expect small kings or "snakes," as they are called; later on, about January, the 30 lb-50 lb "smokers" arrive. The biggest fish are often caught after a cold front when the wind swings into the north and the ocean gets rough. Along the Atlantic coast smaller fish can be found in 40' of water while the larger kings are in 90'-120'; along the Gulf coast fish are found in water ranging up to 40'.

TACKLE

Spinning and Plug Casting. This tackle can be used although it is a bit light. A 6'-7' rod, fairly stiff; 15#-25# line, mono or braided; spin or conventional reel.

Trolling. A 5½' stand-up rod; 300-350 yd of 20#-30# line (or to 80# for trolling large lures), mono or braided; conventional reel.

Jigging. A 5½'-7' rod; 300 yd of 20#-30# line, mono or braided; spin or conventional reel.

Fly. A 8½'-9' rod, 8-10 weight; fast-sinking or sink-tip, weight-forward line; reel with 200 yd of 20# Dacron backing.

Surf and Pier. A 9'-12' medium to heavy rod; 25#-40# line, mono or braided; spin or conventional reel.

TECHNIQUES

Surf and Pier

Artificial Bait. During November and May along the middle stretches of both coasts when there is a lot of bait in the water, kingfish are sometimes in a swash canal within casting distance from shore. Large plugs such as the Magnum Rapala, Rebel Jaw-breaker, 17-series Bomber in chartreuse or black and gold, and the largest Mirrolures will reach these fish. Also try plugs in a mackerel finish, a red head and white body or dark back and white or silver belly. Attach 2'-3' of wire leader made from #5 or #6 coffee-stained stainless. As these artificials provide plenty of attraction on their own, a slow retrieve is all that is necessary.

Live Bait. There is no doubt that live bait consistently takes more fish and the largest ones, too. From shore it is nearly impossible to cast a live fish far enough out to reach kings, but from a pier, one can easily get to them. Fish the swash canals the pier intersects, or go right out to the end—the best spot on the pier for kings. Any live bait will do; the ones you catch with net or hook and line along the pier will of course be livelier than any you bring in from elsewhere.

With a long rod you can swing-cast underhand and you would want to use a 5′ leader made from one piece of #7 wire or 1′ of the wire attached to the hook and 4′ of 80#-100# mono; barrel swivels at both ends of the mono enable you to attach it to both wire and fishing line. The hook should be 6/0-8/0 short shank. If the live bait is a mullet, hook it through the upper lip; if you use a blue runner or other small fish, hook just ahead of the dorsal fin. The most important step is next: attach one or two stingers, which are hooks attached by wire to the eye of the main hook and either lightly hooked in the bait or allowed to swing free. A stinger is the fisherman's answer to the kingfish's habit of striking short, just missing the hook (so close you can't believe it!) and cutting off the back half of the bait. The first stinger can be a single 6/0 or #2 or #3 treble hook that lightly penetrates the skin along the bait's side and the second can be free. If only one stinger is used, it can be attached or free. When a kingfish attacks the bait, allow a second or two before setting the hook. There is a good technique that can be used from the pier end and gets the bait very far out: with an offshore wind blowing, attach a balloon about 6′ above the hook. Freeline the bait out as far as your spool of line will allow and still leave a reserve to fight the fish.

Boat Fishing

Slow Trolling. Using live bait such as mullet, menhaden, pinfish, scaled sardines, etc., hook through the upper lip if a mullet or both lips if any other kind, and use a stinger as explained above. The objective is to troll so that the bait sinks deep and does not spin in the water. Accordingly, the boat should execute zig-zags, circles, figure 8's, and sharp right angles. It may also be necessary to pull a sea anchor or a bucket to slow down enough. Backtrolling is done by a few fishermen: in reverse gear go stern first through the water, the trolled baits and bow of the boat pointing in the same direction.

One can also slow-troll with dead bait such as rigged mullet, ballyhoo, and sardines. Again, use a stinger which, on a small bait, can be the eye of one hook passed over the point and barb of the other and pointed in the opposite direction. If trolling from outriggers, lower the pin to your eye level to reduce the length of drop back. In using flat lines, attach a tag line to the fishing line. This is a 2′ or 3′ piece of heavy line attached at one end to a boat cleat or anything available and at the other end with a cheap clothespin to hold the fishing line. Artificials are effective trolled; try the Magnum Rapala, a Rebel Jawbreaker, and Cairns Swimmers all of which are good in March when winds stir up the waters and reduce visibility. For this kind of trolling a 50#-80# outfit is required. Use a wide circle or spoon wrap to attach the plug to the wire leader, which can be the same as described above.

Deep Trolling. Rigged dead baits can be trolled deep and so can live bait if the boat can travel very slowly. Planers, wire line, downriggers, and just heavy, cigar-shaped weights ahead of the leader will take a bait down to where kingfish are holding. Large bluish or chrome spoons at least 4″ long are effective when fished deep. Attach the spoon to a wire leader with a wide circle and connect the wire to the line with a ball-bearing swivel.

Drift Fishing. Perhaps the most effective method of taking king-fish, drift fishing is how the large, deep-sea fishing or "head" boats operate. One can drift using live or dead bait, but the main ingredient is chum. Throw a cup or two of chum into the water and repeat every several minutes. Fish with any live bait, such as a grunt or a yellowtail snapper that you might catch on light tackle in the same place you have chummed; use two hooks, about 6/0, one through the upper lip and the other hanging free. Large live shrimp, although expensive to buy, are excellent kingfish bait. Or use dead bait such as pieces of menhaden, as the commercial boats do. Try an unweighted bait for the surface water and a weighted one to go a little deeper. When the line is straight out from the drifting boat, reel in a few feet very slowly, lift the rod tip straight up, and slowly lower it. Nighttime drift fishing is the most productive of all; fish while the moon is half full, either waxing or waning, and between 9 and 11 o'clock and an hour or two before and after the first light of dawn. A 4'-6' 40#-80# mono leader plus 8"-10" of #7 wire to guard against a king's sharp teeth is required.

Deep Jigging. When kings have been located, deep jigging is highly successful. It can be done while drifting or while swinging from an anchor placed well upcurrent or upwind of the fishing spot. Using the leader described above, choose the lightest weight jig necessary to get down to the level desired; with light line this might mean 3/4 oz if there is no current while with heavy line, 1 oz or more. A white, bullet-head jig is the best and to it you can attach a ballyhoo. First, break off the bill and then pass the hook of the jig through the upper and then the lower jaw; attach one or more stingers to this hook or to the jig eye. Shrimp, a strip of squid, mullet or other fish, a plastic worm, pork rind or any other such attraction can also be added to a bare jig as they increase its appeal to the fish. Lower the jig to the bottom and raise it a few feet. Then lower the rod tip so slowly that you feel the weight of the jig at all times, and repeat. Retrieve a few feet higher to try at a different water level. Another productive way to jig is to jerk the lure off the bottom so that it jumps up like a frightened baitfish. To do this with a conventional reel, set it in free spool and let the jig hit the bottom while drifting over fish. The instant the line is slack, place your thumb on the spool and lift the rod tip quickly to make the jig jump up; then release your thumb, free spool to the bottom, and repeat. Be careful: when a fish strikes, lift your thumb immediately and throw the reel in gear or you'll end up with, at best, a backlash or, at worst, burnt flesh. With a spin reel you can perform the same maneuver but you must set it in the mode to reel backward which will allow the lure to sink; this avoids fooling with the bail. With either reel, when so much line is out that you can no longer easily tell when the jig hits bottom, reel in and repeat the entire procedure. Also, be alert when you lower the artificial in the first place, as frequently fish grab a free-falling bait.

Fly Fishing. Because it will be hard to get kings to the surface, a sinking line is required. Chum the fish to come as near as possible and cast to them. A white 3″-4″ streamer and a bushy red-brown fly designed to drift in a chum line are both very good.

What To Do About a Cut-off. In spite of a stinger or two, kingfish may get away with part of the bait and no part of the hook. If you feel a sharp tug and then nothing, immediately feed line out and let the bait sink deeper in the water. One hopes that the sight of a sinking fish will prove so attractive that the king will return to finish the meal.

How to Land a Kingfish. Small fish can be swung aboard, directly into the fish box. Large fish can be dangerous: the scar on my elbow is proof. Always gaff a fish over 10 lb and the best place to sink the hook is the heavy region of the back in front of the dorsal fin.

Other Fish Caught While Kingfishing. Sailfish, barracuda, grouper, and occasionally dolphin.

Regulations

- Closed Season: none
- Minimum Size: 20″ from nose to fork of tail
- Maximum Size: no regulation
- Daily Bag Limit: 2

15

Spanish Mackerel
(Scomberomorus maculatus)

This game fish is absolutely first-rate on very light tackle and is excellent for eating. Preferred water temperature: over 68° F. All-tackle record: 13 lb.

WHERE AND WHEN

The entire Florida coast from bays, inlets, and passes to ten miles offshore but, commonly, in 20'-40' of water. Although some Spanish are caught the year around in the northern part of the state, spring and fall are generally the best times, including the winter in the southern end of Florida. Any kind of weather, from the crackling bright days of a calm, winter sea to a cold, howling northeaster can be the right time for Spanish mackerel.

TACKLE

Surf and Inlet. Because Spanish mackerel are a little farther out than other surf fishes, a long surf rod to reach them is necessary: rod to 14'; 20#-40# line, mono or braided; spin or conventional reel. Depending on the width of the inlet, either a surf rod or a spinning or plug casting rod can be used; about a 7' rod; 8#-15# line, mono or braided; spin or conventional reel.

Trolling. Use the spinning or plug casting equipment above or any light trolling outfit.

Fly. A 7-9 weight rod about 8½'; dark, floating, weight-forward or a sink-tip line; a reel with backing of about 100 yd of 12# Dacron.

TECHNIQUES

Boat Fishing

Casting. In calm weather, cruise in depths of 20'-40' in the open ocean or Gulf or in 6'-12' in bays and look for "nervous" water—surface areas stippled by the movement of bait fish and decidedly different from adjacent water. Or in any kind of weather, look for bait fish scattering across the water's surface and for birds circling and diving. When you believe you have found a school of Spanish, approach quietly and throw into their midst chum made up of dead glass minnows or ground-up fish with an occasional handful of glass minnows. When the fish come after the chum, cast into them with live bait or artificials or even with cut chunks of fish. For live bait use a live glass minnow, a scaled sardine, or a pilchard hooked through the lips or in the back ahead of the dorsal fin with a long shank 5/0 hook. For the largest Spanish, a live shrimp hooked through the head is hard to beat. A foot or two of 30# mono or #3 wire as a leader is necessary and a split shot or two above the black swivel connecting leader and line will keep the bait down where the fish are. With artificials, also use a short leader as above and cast with a #3-#6 Clark spoon (many other kinds, as well) or a ¼ oz nylon jig in all white, all yellow, or a red and white combination. Let the artificial sink a few feet and retrieve rapidly while jerking the rod tip. If a striking fish fails to take the hook of a jig, free spool, throw it back into gear, and continue with the retrieve. Where Spanish are surface feeding on ballyhoo, a floating plug such as a Mirrolure 95MR or something similar will catch fish. Whenever you are in a school of Spanish and they refuse your artificials, change to smaller sizes.

Trolling. Fish can be located by trolling with spoons with or without an added strip of fish or squid, about ¼-½ oz jigs in colors as above, and medium-size plugs. Keep the artificial down by adding an egg sinker about an ounce or two ahead of the black swivel. Don't be afraid to troll rapidly, up to 1500 rpm. When you catch a Spanish, anchor the boat if it is shallow enough or drift if it is not, and chum and fish as described under casting above.

Surf and Inlet

Especially in the fall when schools of bait fish are moving south, Spanish mackerel come in close to shore and can be reached by casting live or cut-up bait and artificials. At this time they are often caught by fishermen after bluefish, so refer to that section for directions. But casting any bait as described above will work.

Fly. When they are close to shore or when you chum them up to a boat, a fly rod is a perfect tool for catching Spanish mackerel. Dark line should be used to avoid Spanish or blues striking at and cutting it. For lures try mainly white streamers with a strip of blue, green, or black on the top; red and white streamers; and shrimp imitations. Up to 4' of leader with a 6#-10# tippet plus 1' of 40# shock or 3"-4" of #3 wire attached with an Albright Special knot is necessary. Just as with other ways to catch Spanish, a sink-tip line may be necessary to reach the fish.

Other Fish Caught While Fishing for Spanish Mackerel. Bluefish, jack crevalle, kingfish, barracuda, cero mackerel, and snook.

Regulations

- Closed Season: none
- Minimum Size: 12" from nose to fork of tail
- Maximum Size: no regulation
- Daily Bag Limit: 10
- **Note: Spanish mackerel must be brought in with head and fins intact.**

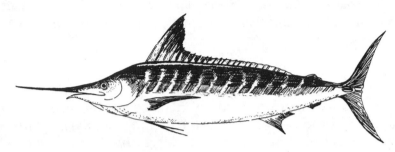

16

Blue Marlin
(*Makaira nigricans*)

This enormous fish puts on a spectacular aerial display as it leaps clear of the water's surface often twenty-five times or more, greyhounds across it with unbelievable speed, or sounds to the depths and refuses to budge. Whatever kind of show it stages, the angler's work is clearly cut out for him when taking on a blue marlin. Although they are excellent for eating, this finest fighter of all the marlins is never numerous and should always be released. Preferred water temperature: 70°–80° F. All-tackle record (in the Atlantic): 1,402 lb 2 oz.

WHERE AND WHEN

1. The "wall," a sharp dropoff in the sea floor 19 miles south of Key West, is considered Florida's best blue marlin spot. Fished year-round, the "wall" produces best late spring to fall, October being very good if there has been some cold weather; by November fish are certain to be there. However, all the Keys produce blue marlin in the spring with a peak in April.
2. The Atlantic coast, especially between Palm Beach and Jupiter, April through July, and the "rolldown," a ledge that

plunges to over 1,000′, 52 miles out from St. Augustine, where the action is good in April, May, and September.

3. The Panhandle along the 100-fathom curve where blues appear as early as May and remain through October.

TACKLE

Trolling. For fish that can reach over half a ton, heavy tackle is generally used. This means at least a 50⌗ or 80⌗ outfit, but 130⌗ is safer and used quite often, too. These sizes are set by the International Game Fish Association (IGFA) which keeps records in these, among other, categories. A 50⌗ outfit, for example, would imply not only 50⌗ line but rod and reel to match. Such "class" or "tournament" tackle, as it is called, means a 6/0-9/0 reel holding at least 600 yd of Dacron line and a stout glass or glass-graphite 7′ rod with roller guides plus often a special butt made of a strong material such as aluminum tubing. Other heavy equipment such as a bucket harness and a fighting chair complete such an outfit, but there are many excellent fishermen who prefer to use a 5½′ stand-up rod for doing battle with giant blue marlin; they need a shoulder harness and fighting belt.

Fly. As incredible as it may seem after reading the foregoing, some anglers have beaten blue marlin with a fly rod. You need a 12 or 13 weight system that includes a reel holding at least 600 yd of Micron backing. There are some fly reels that have a capacity of 1,000 yd. See the fly equipment recommended for sailfish, p. 84.

TECHNIQUES

Ocean Trolling

Natural Bait

Dead bait: Trolling dead fish such as Spanish mackerel, bonefish, mullet, barracuda, or dolphin was a technique used more often in the past than now. The best dead fish most easily procured now is a whole, very fresh Spanish mackerel bought in a fish store. Choose them at about a pound with their yellow spots still showing and very clear eyes. A mackerel's flat body and toughness make for an excellent trolling bait. It should be either belly- or head-rigged, and in areas where much blue marlin fishing occurs, pre-rigged baits can be bought in bait and tackle stores. To use such a bait, doubling the line with a Bimini Twist is considered necessary by some, but not all, fishermen.

There is a feeling that the knot resulting from doubling heavy line will, in a day's fishing, fray going in and out of rod guides and may just pop at the wrong time. But there is less disagreement about leaders: most anglers want as much 300# mono as allowed by the IGFA and still make the catch accept- able as a possible record. The IGFA regulations on tackle over 20# are that a leader used alone cannot exceed 30' and, if combined with a double line, the total cannot exceed 40'. To fasten such heavy mono to a hook or to make a loop in the other end is no job for a knot, no matter which kind; only crimping a metal sleeve or two in tandem around the mono will work. This means, then, for those anglers who do not double their line, the only possible weak link in the entire rig is the improved clinch knot attaching a heavy snap swivel to the Dacron line. Such a dead bait is fished from both outriggers and flat lines. Reel drags are set to 1/3 of the line's breaking strength. Search for rare blue marlin anywhere in the open ocean, a current rip with or without weeds, or under circling birds. Dropoffs such as already mentioned are prime locations. The western edge of the Gulf Stream is the general locality where blues roam and this gets farther and farther from shore as you proceed up the Atlantic coast: from a couple of miles out in South Florida to 40-50 miles out off Daytona Beach. While fishing, always be on the lookout for a blue "tailing" through the water surface.

Live bait: Although not much water is covered by slow-trolling live fishes, this may be the most effective method of catching blue marlin, especially when you know they are around. Pro- ductive days occur when the current runs strong and the blue of the Gulf Stream water is clear and clean. The best live bait is a 10-lb bonito (little tunny) caught with a hand-line baited with a spoon or feather. Also school dolphin, caught as des- cribed in the chapter on dolphin, are excellent live bait. After capturing one of these, the main problem is keeping it alive and frisky throughout the rigging process, not an easy task. First place the fish just caught in a wet towel belly-up; it can be held by one person while another attaches the hook. Running saltwater through a hose into the fish's mouth helps. Next find the eye socket, a small passageway through the head. If you look at the right side of the fish's head, you will see this cavity in the one o'clock position relative to the eye; from the left side it appears in the eleven o'clock position. You should have a Dacron bridle ready to use, and this may be accomplished several ways.

The easiest is to tie, using any knot, the middle of a 10″ piece of 50# Dacron to the bend of a 10/0-14/0 marlin hook that has already been connected by crimping to a 300# mono leader. Then, with an open-eyed rigging needle attached to one end of the line, pass it all the way through the eye socket. Position the hook so that the shank points straight ahead of the bait with the bend between the eyes and the point straight up. Tie the two ends of Dacron to secure the hook to the head. All this should take only a few seconds to ensure that the bait will be lively when put into the water. This is possible by practicing with dead bait and making certain everything is ready when a bait fish is caught.

The bonito or dolphin can be trolled from outrigger or flat line at dead slow speed, meaning that the motor must be placed in and out of gear quite often to slow down the boat. If you are short-handed or have not yet mastered the art of rigging a live bait, you can proceed another way: pre-rig a 12/0-14/0 hook by crimping a loop of 300# mono leader to its eye. With a heavy split ring connect it at the bend to the eye of a 6/0 or 8/0 hook. Pass the smaller hook into the bait's mouth and out through the top of its head. Another technique, especially above a school of dolphin below which blue marlin frequently lie in wait, is to send a live bait deep on a downrigger.

Artificial Bait. Although the debate about whether artificials are more deadly than live bait with blue marlin goes on and on, one thing is certain: far more territory can be covered moving up to 16 knots than trolling slowly to keep a bait alive and natural-looking. This is especially important when one considers that blue marlin are relatively scarce and fishing a large area is often necessary. And there is even more debate over which artificials are the most effective. Lures work by attracting fish in a unique fashion, some erratically moving through the water as light reflects from their mirrored sides and others leaving a bubble trail 50'-75' behind. Lure manufacturers constantly try to come up with variations; whether an Iland, a Moldcraft, a Konahead, a C & H, or a Schneider or whether it should be 8" or 15" long, no one can say with certainty which is best, but 7"-12" lures are currently in vogue. And that is not even to mention colors which are as mixed as the imagination allows. For a starting guideline, find out the manufacturer's recommended speed for the lure you use as some perform best going slowly while with others you need to race through the water. Color combinations that have produced over the years are black and red, purple and pearl, blue and white, yellow and white, and pink and white. In some places blue marlin seem to prefer only certain colors; for example, at the "wall" off Key West, red and white, orange and yellow, and all black are the colors to use. Also, some fishermen make certain to use dark lures on overcast days and light-colored ones when it's sunny. Sometimes a ballyhoo is rigged so that the lure completely covers it and does not interfere with rapid trolling. A most effective technique is to attach one or more "birds" ahead of the lure; these short-winged airplane-shaped teasers leap in and out of the water giving the impression of a school of fish. They are placed where desired on the mono leader and a metal sleeve crimped just behind where they should remain. The addition of another teaser, one about the size of a bowling pin with a painted bonito finish, is often run close astern on its own hand line. Lures are often double-hooked, the connection being 450# cable; the second hook can hang free or can be rigged in such a way that it rides at a ninety degree angle to the first. Leaders are 300# or 400# mono and are secured by metal crimps. All these mate-rials — rigged and ready to use — can be bought at bait and tackle stores. To troll artificials, use an outrigger or flat line, and place each lure on the front face of one of the waves coming off the side and stern behind the moving boat, so that they are not only spread out in different locations but are staggered in distance out. One additional refinement is a result of the dropback and the slack line that occurs when a fish "knocks down" a bait from the outrigger pin. The problem is that when the blue (or any fish, for that matter) discovers that in its mouth is not a real fish but a piece of plastic or whatever, it will drop the bait and run. To shorten the dropback and therefore the time a fish has to make this decision, use a tag line—a piece of line attached to the outrigger pin on one end and the fishing line at the other. Usually 400# mono or Dacron about the length of the outrigger is crimped on to the outrigger release clip and at the free end is attached a 200# test snap swivel. Connect this to a fishing line just beyond the rod tip after the bait has been let out and placed. The easiest way to make this attachment is to wrap a #64 rubber band several times around the fishing line and pass its end under one of the loops it has made; secure this in the snap swivel at the end of the tag line. Put the reel in free spool which then raises the tag line to the height from which the lure swims best. On a strike there is one danger: the swivel may backlash into the cockpit, a potentially dangerous situation that can be nullified by using stiff outriggers. On the flip side, after a strike the tag line clip usually ends up in the cockpit and one can set up again without fooling with the outrigger halyard.

Fly. Fly fishing for creatures as large as blue marlin is not for everyone but it has been done successfully and the record is a 203 lb 8 oz fish. Because of the blue marlin's surface acrobatics, it is difficult to imagine that with IGFA tackle limitations a larger fish will be caught on a fly rod. The technique is the same as for fly rodding for sailfish and can be read in that section, p. 89. Naturally, class tippets should be the strongest the IGFA allows: 20# plus 12" of shock tippet made of 100# mono. Flies and popping bugs are used as suggested for sailfish.

How to Hook a Blue Marlin. As a blue marlin approaches to feed, the alert angler, whose eyes have been glued to the baits since they were put out, usually sees a sudden change in fish color from a dirty gray or brown—somewhat resembling a shark for a moment—to a deep black or neon-blue as the fish strikes. If none of this happens and the blue simply swims behind the baits as if looking them over, turn the boat slightly in one direction and then another to see if the change provokes a strike. When a blue hits an artificial lure, a hook-up should immediately result because of the tag line. But if the fish misses, continue on the same course and alter neither speed nor direction. If the fish connects, set the hook hard two or three times. On a natural bait knock-down, put the reel in free spool (or set it this way in the beginning with only the click on to prevent line from blowing off the spool) with your thumb lightly on the turning spool to prevent a tangle. When the spool picks up speed, throw the reel in gear, wait for the line to come taut, and set the hook as above. At the same time you set, the boat operator should gun the motor ahead to help guarantee the hook will stick. If the fish is not on, reel in to bring the bait back to where it was and return to trolling speed; perhaps the blue will try again.

How to Land a Blue Marlin. A couple of hundred pounds of muscle attached to a dangerous bill at boatside constitutes a threat to life. To begin with, the fish should have been fought to exhaustion (the fish's, although possibly the angler's, too). From a seated position in a fighting chair, line can be pulled in by one gloved hand while the other cranks the reel handle; with a stand-up rod, steady pumping should gradually bring a tired fish to boatside. If, at this point, you have incorrectly estimated the fish's condition and it begins another run, the drag must be loosened immediately and the fighting begun once again. When the fish is close enough, if it is to be released, the leader is clipped. If it is to be brought aboard, there are two methods and each requires a person or two aboard in addition to angler and boat handler. The methods are the flying gaff and tail rope. The large flying gaff is sunk into the fish's shoulder region and the metal hook separates from the long handle. A line connecting the hook to a cleat keeps the fish close-by. When its head can be raised, a heavy billy club is used, the target being the skull between and behind the eyes. A tail rope is a stiff rope with one end made fast to a cleat while the other is placed around the leader and snapped shut to form a loop; this is passed over the fish down to the tail and drawn tight. The boat is gunned ahead and the leader let go; the fish is towed backwards to drown in a minute or two.

Other Fish Caught While Fishing for Blue Marlin. White marlin, dolphin, wahoo, tunas, and sailfish.

Regulations

- Closed Season: none
- Minimum Size: 86″ tip of lower jaw to fork in tail
- Maximum Size: no regulation
- Daily Bag Limit: one per day of any billfish

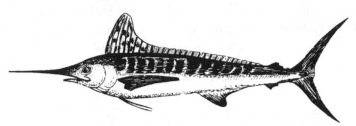

17

White Marlin; Spikefish
(Tetrapturus albidus)

Known for its acrobatics — especially greyhounding across the water's surface — and for its neon-blue color as it prepares to take a bait, the white marlin is a highly prized Florida game fish that is most often caught while sailfishing. Although they taste very good smoked, whites are nearly always released. Preferred water temperature: 70°-85° F. All-tackle record: 181 lb 14 oz.

WHERE AND WHEN

1. Southeast Florida, from the end of February to the middle of May, especially when the wind has been blowing east or northeast for a few days and blue Gulf Stream water is close in and making a sharp edge with green, inshore water.
2. The Keys, March through May, usually around schools of dolphin.
3. The Panhandle, along the 100-fathom curve, from September to November.

TACKLE

Trolling and Live Bait. The same as for sailfish, p. 84.

Fly. The same as for sailfish, p. 84.

TECHNIQUES

Ocean Trolling. Fishing for white marlin is fishing for sailfish: you might catch one or the other since the techniques are the same. The main difference is that white marlin might be anywhere in the ocean from water 50′ deep to many miles offshore. Also, whites don't flush as easily as sailfish: they will return to a bait or go from one bait to another even though it is certain they have noticed a hook is partially hidden in the bait. If one were out fishing only for whites—an unlikely thing to do—then a slightly larger bait such as a 10″ mullet or a strip about the same length might be used. Because they sometimes travel in schools, the only time one might actively pursue whites is when some have been recently caught in the vicinity. Artificial lures, a little smaller than those used for blue marlin, will catch whites but they are not nearly as effective as the sailfish techniques described in that section.

Fly. The same as for sailfish, p. 89.

How to Hook a White Marlin. A difference between white marlin and other billfish is that they require a very short dropback, almost none at all. Tag lines, as described in the blue marlin section, can be used but the best solution is for the angler to take care of the dropback himself. When a white hits the bait, throw the reel in gear, point the rod tip at the fish, feel its weight, and set the hook. All of this should happen in no more than three or four seconds. If the fish is not on the hook, raise the rod tip high and jig it slightly; when the fish again takes the bait, just lower the tip, point it at the fish, and set the hook. Sometimes plunging the rod tip into the water will tempt a following, reluctant white into striking. The interesting thing is that unlike sailfish, whites keep coming back after the bait and often need time and coaxing before they strike it.

How to Land a White Marlin. The same as for sailfish, p. 91.

Other Fish Caught While Fishing for White Marlin. The same as for sailfish, p. 91.

Regulations

- Closed Season: none
- Minimum Size: 62" tip of lower jaw to fork in tail
- Maximum Size: no regulation
- Daily Bag Limit: one per day of any billfish

18

Permit; Round Pompano; Great Pompano
(Trachinotus falcatus)

In terms of intelligence, great bursts of speed, and difficulty in catching, especially with fly tackle, the permit is at the top of most fishermen's lists. It is excellent to eat but is nearly always released. Preferred water temperature: 72°–84° F. All-tackle record: 53 lb 4 oz.

WHERE AND WHEN

1. Atlantic coast, primarily in the Keys from Biscayne Bay down, with the best area from Newfound Harbor to the Marquesas Keys. However, such places as the Blue Hole, a 131′ depression about 40 miles from Key West and Lake Worth, where the all-tackle record permit was caught, are possibilities for very large fish. Fishing is best during the new and full moons from late April through November with the peak times near the beginning and the end of this period. The peak period in the Marquesas flats is March and April. The best time to fish permit is when it is windy, blowing 15-20 mph: to be in the lee, where casting is easy

and where the fish will come close in, you must be on the Gulf side when it blows east or southeast and on the Atlantic side if it blows north or northeast. Generally found on hard, coral-bottom flats, in depressions in the flats, and in the deeper water along the flats' edges, permit feed on a flood tide. They swim from deeper water on to the flats as soon as there is 3'-4' of depth, grubbing the bottom for food as they muddy it while at the same time lifting their tails out of water; both are signs of feeding fish. Deeper areas around Keys' bridges are productive, especially during the last two hours of ebb tide. Because of the heat in the shallow Keys water, the best fishing is always in the early morning or late afternoon; in midsummer, the cool of deeper water is an additional requirement. Also, there is good fishing around Key West wrecks beginning in June.

2. Gulf coast, especially the wrecks north of Key West and the flats in the Content Keys area. In addition, some 25-50 miles offshore of the Marco to Boca Grande area there are wrecks, artificial reefs, and freshwater springs (the locations of which are kept very secret) that produce large permit, especially May through September. Other factors to consider are the same as for permit on the Atlantic side.

TACKLE

Spinning and Plug Casting. At least an 8' rod for long casts because permit are easily flushed; 8#-10# line, mono or braided; spin or conventional reel.

Fly. A 8½'-9½' 8-10 weight rod; weight-forward floating or sink-tip line; reel with at least 200 yd of 20# Dacron backing.

TECHNIQUES

Flats

Natural Bait. Most permit have been taken on spin and plug casting outfits while using natural bait. Although shrimp, squid, conch, fiddler crabs, and cut-up lobster have caught permit, the best bait by far is a live, 3" across-the-back crab which may be blue, green, or brown. They can be bought or caught at low tide on the flats with a small minnow net. Or they can be dipped out of flowing ebb tide water in Gulf coast passes, especially Boca Grande. Remove the claws, if you wish, and, using a bronze short shank Mustad 9175 or a Wright and McGill #254 hook about 2/0 or 3/0 in size, pass the hook point up from the crab's bottom through the top shell at the edge where the shell comes to a point. Re-hone the hook now to make it extremely sharp.

Use a 2′-3′ leader of 20#-30# mono and double the fishing line with a Bimini Twist for about 4′ or 5′. Wading the flats for permit is exciting and highly recommended but there is a problem: a large hooked fish will swim too fast for you to follow and recapture or untangle line. Probably fishing from a flats skiff is a better way to start. At any rate, when a fish is in your sights, cast a few yards beyond it and let the crab land gently; the trick at this point is not to flush the fish. Raise the rod tip high in the air and retrieve the crab across the water's surface. When a permit sees the bait and swims after it, stop everything; lower the rod tip, let the crab sink to the bottom, and put the reel in free spool. When the permit grabs the bait and turns, wait a second or two, throw the reel in gear, wait for the line to tighten, and set the hook two or three times. Live shrimp hooked through the head are alright but only if you can't catch or buy crabs. Cast a shrimp near a feeding permit and skitter it across the surface, lower the rod tip, let it sink, and wait. Or, continue skittering the shrimp and stop when a fish sees it and turns. While on the flats be on the lookout for rays as permit are often nearby and for some reason are less likely to flush at your cast. Mudding permit are also more approachable than at other times.

Artificial Bait. Spinning equipment is necessary to cast the light lures that have taken permit on the flats. Double the fishing line and use a leader as with natural bait and cast to a sighted fish. Retrieve the lure in short jerks and, when the fish sees it, let the jig sink to the bottom and remain motionless. When the permit reaches the lure, make one long sweeping retrieval and, when the fish is felt, strike hard as above. Use a Nickelure Popeye, ¼-⅜ oz; or any skimmer-type jig. The best colors are white, sand, tan, pink, and red and white.

Deep Water

Permit, as with other fishes, find wrecks and artificial reefs attractive, particularly during the summer months. If fishing near such structure, establish its position with a marker and set an anchor upcurrent of this place. Drop back over the wreck and fish deep by jigging with a white jig up to 2 oz tipped with a small piece of shrimp or, if using very light tackle, a skimmer-type flats jig as previously discussed. Chumming with shrimp helps and a crab as bait here, as on the flats, is the permit's favorite. If fishing in a channel or in deep water along a bridge, pick a spot where there is a strong tide and you can see weed coming up to the surface. Float a live crab or shrimp downcurrent with the reel set in free spool so there is nothing holding on to the bait to make it look unnatural. Allow a striking fish to run off with the bait a second or two, throw the reel in gear, and set the hook.

Fly Fishing

Fishermen should realize that permit are one of the most difficult fish to catch on a fly; the following directions are known to have worked but bear in mind that this is tough fishing and an experimental nature is a required part of a permit fisherman's arsenal. A 12'-14' leader with a tippet not more than 12# is necessary. Starting with a Ragland Puff fly, cast a yard ahead of and to the side of a feeding fish and retrieve rapidly with a combination of long and short strips that make the fly travel from the bottom to the surface; this puffs up the sand and attracts permit. When a fish swims for the fly, continue with a long, slow strip and when it strikes, set the hook hard. Or use one of the many varieties of crab-imitation flies: the McCrab or John Montague's patterns are good. They are large and wind resistant so at least a 10 weight system is necessary to cast a 2/0, for example. Also, the mother of epoxy (MOE) flies, diamond-shaped and flat-bodied, are considered excellent flies for permit. With these, cast where you think a moving fish will see the fly and allow it to settle to the bottom. Then a few short strips should send up sand puffs which will entice a permit into striking.

How to Fight a Permit. If the hook has been set hard and is solidly placed in the permit's mouth, the fisherman can expect long, hard, head-shaking runs. For large fish not only is a boat necessary to chase down the fish and recapture line but a boat operator as well: you will be busy enough with the fish.

Other Fish Caught While Fishing for Permit. On the flats: bonefish and barracuda; in deep water: jack crevalle, snappers, grouper, and amberjack.

Regulations

- Closed Season: none
- Minimum Size: 10″ from nose to fork in tail
- Maximum Size: 20″ from nose to fork in tail
- Daily Bag Limit: 10 (this includes both pompano and permit; one may be over 20″)

19

Pompano

(Trachinotus carolinus)

A very scrappy shallow-water fish that is a finicky eater, pompanos are always a challenge to catch. These fish are great for eating. Preferred water temperature: 82°-89° F. All-tackle record: 8 lb 1 oz.

WHERE AND WHEN

1. Entire Atlantic coast but primarily from New Smyrna south to Miami. October to December and April to July are the best months but the fisherman should keep in mind that pompano move out into deep water when it is cold and only appear in the surf during warm weather. They may be caught while surf and pier fishing at such prime fishing spots as Playalinda Beach between New Smyrna and Titusville, Juno Beach just below Jupiter, and the surf between Melbourne and Sebastian Inlet. Fish the sloughs, swash canals, and any deeper water along a sand bar. Flood tide, early in the morning, dusk, clean water and a northeast to southeast wind up to 20 mph are considered prime conditions; if it blows for a few days, then is calm for a day or two, and the wind starts in again, go fishing. But don't hesitate to

try at any time of a windless day as pompano are caught
then, too. They are also found during ebb tide in inlets and
bodies of water near inlets such as Lake Worth Inlet and
Lake Worth at Palm Beach; St. Lucie Inlet and the Crossroads near Stuart; and other, smaller inlets along the coast
such as Boynton, Boca Raton, etc.

2. Entire Gulf coast, especially St. Petersburg to Fort Myers,
    and more precisely Anna Maria Island near Tampa Bay; also
    beaches in the Panhandle in late February, a fall run in cuts
    at Apalachicola Bay and the surf nearby are good pompano
    locations. The information about wind conditions, etc. on
    the Atlantic coast applies here, too.

TACKLE

Spinning and Plug Casting. For inshore waters and when the fish
are close to shore, a 7' rod; 4#-8# line, mono or braided; spin or
conventional reel.

Surf. An 8'-14' surf rod; 20#-30# line, mono or braided; spin
or conventional reel.

Fly. A 7 weight rod, 8½'-9'; reel holding 100 yd of 20# Dacron
backing; shooting head, fast sinking line.

TECHNIQUES

Surf, Pier, Inlet, and Inshore

Natural Bait

Sand fleas: More accurately (but not locally) known as a mole
   crab, this crustacean that burrows into the sand as a wave
   recedes is the best obtainable bait. Catch them with a flea trap,
   a rectangular-shaped container covered by a metal screen on
   all but one side and attached to a wooden dowel or PVC pipe.
   Pull the trap in the surf as the waves stir up the sand, or, when it
   is calm, scoop up the top few inches of sand at the water's edge
   to 6'-8' out. Without a trap, a shovel or just hands and fast legs
   will work if the area exposed by a retreating wave is searched.
   They may also be bought alive or frozen in bait and tackle

stores. Keep sand fleas alive while fishing by placing them in a small canvas sack and dunk in seawater often. They can be kept overnight in damp sand in a cool place. Make up a pompano rig by tying two or three small loops about 6" apart in a 3' piece of 30# mono. Attach it to the fishing line with a double surgeon's knot and at the other end, using an improved clinch knot, connect a pyramid sinker from 3-6 oz, depending on the size rod used and the size of the surf. Thread orange beads on the hook loops and attach wide-gap 1/0 hooks to each. Impale the sand flea by working the hook point into the triangular digger on its bottom side and then out through the back. If fleas are small, two or three can be used. Cast to places where water from a receding wave moves especially fast and set the rod in a sand spike which can be bought or made from PVC pipe. As the waves slowly move your rigs shoreward, reel in slack line. Pompano fishermen usually fish two or three rods at the same time.

Clams: In the Melbourne-Sebastian area, clams from the inshore water nearby are commonly used and sometimes catch more fish than sand fleas. Break one open, trim away the soft parts, use all the tough meaty section or cut it into two pieces, and thread the hook with one of these. Use the same rig as with sand fleas. An especially productive bait is a combination on one hook of both a sand flea and a piece of clam.

Shrimp: Probably used more when inshore fishing for pompano, live ones are best but fresh dead shrimp that are peeled will do. Shrimp and clams when frozen together make a very good bait. Rig as with sand fleas if pieces are used; if whole, live shrimp are your bait, a one or two hook-rig is enough.

Artificial Bait

Spin, plug, and light surf rod: Use a ⅜-½ oz jig that has a red or yellow bullet-shaped head and stiff yellow or yellow-with-red nylon hair that ends at the bend of the hook. In addition, chartreuse, yellow, or white feathers, bucktails, and jigs with plastic tails (especially gold- and silver-flecked shad tails) with or without a piece of shrimp or a small sand flea on the hook are also good artificials. Cast blind or, better yet, spot the fish in clear water from a pier or the surf and cast ahead of and beyond it. Let the jig sink and retrieve by twitching the rod tip sharply upward every four or five seconds; the goal is to bounce the jig off the bottom and send up a puff of sand. Use a 20#-30# mono leader (heavier if you don't want mackerel cut-offs) short enough to make casting comfortable.

Fly: Construct a leader up to 7' made up of 2'-4' 25#, 1½'-2' 12#-16# tippet, and 1' 30# shock. Use weighted flies such as a small white or chartreuse streamer; an Integration, #2 hook; a Mickey Finn, 3/0-5/0 hook; and a commercially-made fly that looks like a sand flea.

How to Hook a Pompano. When using natural bait, strike hard as the fish takes the bait. If a sand spike is used and if it is open in the back, with one arm move the rod sharply back in a long arc, remove it from the holder, take up slack line, and strike again. When jigging with an artificial, set the hook at the slightest tug. When landing the fish in the surf, wait for a wave to help wash the exhausted fish up on the sand—don't try to pull in a fish caught by a receding wave.

Other Fish Caught While Fishing for Pompano. Whiting, catfish, mackerel, and bluefish.

Regulations

- Closed Season: none
- Minimum Size: 10″ from tip of snout to fork in tail
- Maximum Size: 20″ from tip of snout to fork in tail
- Daily Bag Limit: 10 (including permit)
- Note: Pompano must be brought in with head and fins intact.

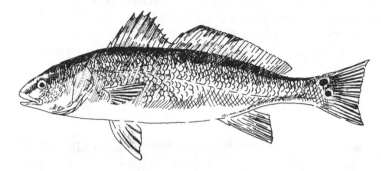

20

Redfish; Channel Bass; Red Drum
(Sciaenops ocellatus)

A very strong fish with great pulling and surging power, redfish make no long runs and are fine for light tackle, especially when casting to sighted fish. Sometimes they can be found in large schools, their bronze bodies seeming to color the water a near pink. The fish are fairly good for eating. Preferred water temperature: 56°-84° F. All-tackle record: 94 lb 2 oz.

WHERE AND WHEN

1. Southwestern coast especially the Ten Thousand Islands and Flamingo areas. Redfish can be caught all year but September, October, and November are the best months. The best times of the month are before, during, and after spring tides. The places to fish the tides are:

- Low slack: deep holes, edges of bars at dropoffs.
- Flood: outside around islands, oyster and sand bars, along mangroves, over shell, rock or sand bottom.
- High slack: outside islands, inside bays along shorelines, open water bars coming to a point.
- Ebb: passes, creeks, and coastal rivers.

2. Entire Gulf coast to the Panhandle. Redfish are available all year, but the times and places that are especially productive are the Cedar Keys in September through December; Charlotte Harbor and Pine Island areas in September through November; the bars and channels in Tampa Bay in the late summer and early fall; Homosassa and Suwannee River tidal creeks in June through December but especially during September and October; Gulf passes such as Boca Grande, Big Carlos, and Captiva during the fall; and the Cape San Blas area and Apalachicola Bay in October. Fish as above over grassy areas that have white sand patches. The best time is a couple of hours before high tide to a couple of hours into the ebb tide.

3. Entire Atlantic coast south to around Jupiter; South Biscayne Bay around to Florida Bay; Nassau River and Sound north of Mayport in the northeast; Mosquito Lagoon near Oak Hill; Sebastian Inlet; and beaches from Cocoa to Vero Beach. September, October, and into November and February through May are prime times. The largest fish in the state are found in these areas. Fish these tides in these locations:

- Inlets: off jetties, inside around oyster bars; ebb tide and nighttime are best.
- Indian and Banana rivers: canals, flats, oyster beds; any tide, but when the tide is very high, try the shallows of flooded marshes.
- Surf: in sloughs during flood tide.

TACKLE

Spinning and Plug Casting. A rod to 7'; 8#-15# line, mono or braided; spin or conventional reel.

Surf. A medium to heavy rod, 10'-14'; 25#-36# line, mono or braided; spin or conventional reel.

Fly. A rod 8½'-9' 8 or 9 weight; floating or sink-tip line; if windy or using large flies, rod and line to 10 weight.

TECHNIQUES

Inlets

Natural Bait. Use a live bait fish, preferably a finger mullet or a large shrimp on a sliding sinker bottom rig. Use 1 oz-5 oz of lead depending on the strength of the current, the objective being to keep the bait on the bottom.

Artificial Bait. Large plugs and large white jigs with a built-in red streak or with a red plastic worm attached are commonly used. Tackle can range up to surf rod size. Use the Atom 40 or Atom Jr.; a Gibbs; or a Magnum Rapala.

Surf

Natural Bait. Use a fish finder rig with up to a 6-oz pyramid lead sinker and bait with cut pieces of mullet.

Artificial Bait. The same as in inlets.

Other Locations

Natural Bait

Shrimp: Thread a cone-shaped, weighted popping cork on the line and tie on a black swivel using an improved clinch knot. Attach a mono leader of 20#-40# (heavier where there are oysters) to the swivel also with an improved clinch knot; the leader should be long enough so that the bait will just reach the bottom. A sliding egg sinker about ½ oz can be placed above the hook to keep the bait down. With the same knot once again, attach to the leader's end a 2/0 long shank hook. Twist off the paddle-like tail of a live or recently dead shrimp and thread it on the hook, starting at the tail and coming out through the shell on the upper back. Adjust the cork so that the bait will be just off the bottom and cast so that the current carries the shrimp under mangroves, near bars, into potholes, or 2'-3' in front of a feeding fish. Pop the cork (loudly in water 3'-5' deep, quietly in shallower water) every few seconds and slowly retrieve, and cast once again. Chum with cut-up bits of shrimp, crab, etc. During low tide watch for tailing fish and approach them very quietly.

Crab: Remove the claws from any kind of crab and hook it through either tip on the side of the shell. Use the rig as above for shrimp.

Fish: Use any live baitfish but pinfish are the best (in the Oak Hill area, use a 3½"-4" pigfish or a shrimp). The shrimp rig described above but without a cork is generally used. Strips of mullet or pieces of any fish are all right but in this case, do use a popping cork. Chum is a good idea if thrown to a spot where redfish are likely to appear.

Artificial Bait

Spin and plug: Double the fishing line with a Bimini Twist loop as long as the fishing rod. With or without a swivel (attach mono to mono with a double surgeon's knot) attach a 1' leader made of up to 40# mono. With floating lures, cast just beyond a redfish and retrieve noisily and slowly, close to the fish's head. Because spoons sink, cast one 10' in front of a sighted fish and retrieve by the fish's head. With jigs, bounce off the bottom in a slow retrieve. Long casts may be necessary as redfish spook easily, so keep the boat a distance away. Use a ½ oz gold spoon such as the Sprite, Acetta Hobo, or Johnson Silver Minnow, and to each add a short plastic tail in pink or red and/or a dab of red fingernail polish on both sides of the front end; a Mirrolure 7M, 44M, 88M, 12M chugger, and 52M (to go deeper as when fishing the larger passes), all with dark backs; a Boone Castana and Spinana; a Bagley Finger Mullet; a Texas-rigged red plastic worm or a rootbeer colored 3"-4" Burke Hookworm; a Cotee green firetail grub; a white or chartreuse bucktail or nylon jig, ¼ oz-⅜ oz, with or without a fingernail-size piece of shrimp on the hook or with or without a plastic tail. Casting a noisy plug such as the chugger above into a deep pothole can bring fish out as nothing else can.

Trolling: Troll with equipment already discussed. Use a 4/0 Barracuda spoon; a Reflecto spoon; a gold Johnson Silver Minnow, ½ oz, with or without a plastic tail, the curly type best, in red or yellow.

Fly: To avoid picking up weed when fly-rodding on the flats, use a knotless, commercially made 9' leader with an added tippet of 8#-12# with another 12" of 20#-30# mono as a shock leader for large fish. Or make one as follows: 4' 25#-30#, 3' 20#, 2' 15#, 1' 12#, 1' 30#-40# shock. Use a popper; a Bend Back River Shrimp; a chartreuse epoxy fly; a white Dahlberg Diver; a Wobbler fly; a Chico's Bend Back in orange and yellow, 1/0-3/0 hook; a Deceiver; a Seaducer in red and white, red and yellow, and red and orange. 1/0-3/0 hook; and in the southwest a Gold Lizzie fly along the mangroves. Bottled fish scent sprayed on flies helps. A fly should be placed in eyesight of a tailing fish. Let it sink and when the red is nearby, begin to retrieve slowly in 3" or 4" strips. As the fish goes for it, retrieve a long strip and when it is on, set the hook by swinging the rod tip sharply to the side. If using a popper, twitch it slightly and don't repeat until the water settles. If a fish appears interested, increase the twitches.

How to Hook a Redfish. When a redfish strikes, don't set the hook immediately upon feeling the fish at the end of the line. Allow it to turn and begin to pull before hauling back for the strike.

Other Fish Caught While Redfishing. Trout, bluefish, and snook.

Regulations

- Closed Season: none
- Minimum Size: 18" overall
- Maximum Size: 27" overall
- Daily Bag Limit: 1

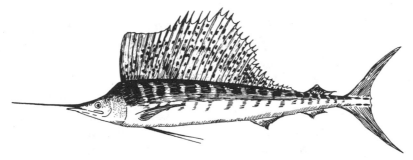

21

Sailfish; Sail; Spindlebeak
(Istiophorus platypterus)

A beautiful and powerful fish capable of swimming up to 70 mph. Its aerial display of jumping and tail-walking 50 feet across the water's surface is not for the faint-hearted. They are sometimes found in large schools. Sailfish taste excellent smoked but are nearly always released. Preferred water temperature: 77°–82° F. All-tackle record: 141 lb 1 oz (Atlantic record).

WHERE AND WHEN

1. South Atlantic coast, especially the Stuart area, has long been the sailfish center of Florida even though in the last few years it has fallen off. November through early March but also summer, especially July, are good times to fish. Many sailfish are caught inside the Gulf Stream in the green, inshore current and along the Continental Shelf; water from about 100'-150' deep is usually considered the correct depth. However, some are caught close in to shore at fishing piers while others are out in the blue water of the Gulf Stream. Fishing any time of the day is possible but mid-day is usually slow. A strong, north-moving current

plus a brisk wind from the north is the best combination of conditions, but the ocean will be rough. During the winter a cold front will trigger sailfish to school and swim south, "tailing" en route.

2. Middle Keys, especially the Islamorada area. Fishing is best November through February, especially December and January, during strong northeast or north winds. These sailfish are caught in 10'-40' of water on a reef with a sharp dropoff such as Alligator, Careysfort, Molasses, Conch, Tennessee, Sombrero, and Looe Reefs. Morning and late afternoon are the best times. In this area sailfish are also caught farther out as described above for the southeast coast.

3. North and central Atlantic coast, summer and early fall, in the Gulf Stream and, in the last few years, as close in as the mouth of the St. Johns River. Generally, however, from Fort Pierce up, one is out of sight of land when sailfishing and the distance increases the farther north one fishes; at St. Augustine the optimal distance is about 52 miles offshore.

4. Panhandle, especially off Destin at the 100 fathom curve. Summer and fall are the best times, July and October being the peak months.

TACKLE

Spinning and Plug Casting. Not generally used except as noted below under Keys fishing. A 7' rod; 12#-15# line, mono or braided; spin or conventional reel.

Trolling and Live Bait. A 30# outfit, mono or braided line, and a 4/0 conventional reel; a rod from 5½' stand-up type to 7' conventional.

Fly. A 9'-9½' rod 11 or 12 weight (with fighting butt) and a floating saltwater taper or weight-forward line to match (or a similar sinking shooting head with 30# shooting line cut down to 25' for less resistance when a fish leaps out of the water); 100' of 25# mono as a shock absorber attached ahead of the backing; 30# Dacron backing, at least 250 and up to 500 yd; and a reel with an absolutely smooth drag system..

TECHNIQUES

Ocean Trolling

The usual technique of trolling is to pull a dead bait or artificial lure through the water so that it looks alive to a sailfish. To accomplish this, always put rigged and ready baits out in the water 10'-15' and pull them along to determine if they swim properly. If they do not, reel them back in and try limbering the bait by bending the body at right angles one way and then the other. If the hook binds against the flesh, cut the slit in the bait's belly slightly larger. Then check the baits in the water again and drop them back to trolling position—about 60' out if from outriggers and half that for flat lines. The main criterion is that the baits should be no farther back than you can easily see them and a fish on the attack. The baits should swim through the water most of the time but occasionally come to the surface and skip. Variables affecting the action of baits in the water are the conditions of the ocean, the wind, the speed of the boat, currents, and whether the bait is being pulled from high up, as from the outrigger, or only a couple of feet above sea level, as with the flat line.

The part of the ocean to troll is inside the Gulf Stream in the green water. If the water is dirty or if the current is from the south, find clean green water in the direction from which the current flows. If none can be found, go out into the blue water. Fish the inshore side of rips and look for fish signs such as diving birds, flying fish, and weedlines. An onshore breeze with a light to medium chop on the water are considered good. The boat should angle left and right, make sharp right-angle turns, and do figure 8's every several minutes.

Sailfish use their bills in a school of bait to stun many in a short time. On a single bait when the sail opens its mouth to take, it only looks like it is using the bill to hit the bait. If a sailfish comes up on a bait, don't change anything until it is hooked. Trolling is sometimes improved by pulling a teaser: it can be the daisy-chain type made with several plastic squids or plastic skirts; a Sea Witch over a hookless bait; a large wooden hookless plug; or even a beverage can with holes at both ends.

Dead Bait

Keeping bait fresh: Bait bought frozen should be allowed to thaw slowly while packed in shaved ice. Bait caught or bought fresh should be sprinkled with kosher or pickling salt and packed in shaved ice: a layer of ice, a layer of fish, etc. A proper drain system is necessary so that bait are never lying in liquid. Fresh bait (either after thawing or if bought) have clear eyes, shiny skins, and hard bellies.

Mullet: Silver mullet 7"-8" or longer have probably caught more sailfish than any other bait along the southeast coast of Florida. One can buy them fresh or frozen or cast net them as discussed in the section on bait. Use a 7/0 or 8/0 hook, a 6' 50# mono leader or a 9' coffee-stained stainless leader, size 5, 6, or 7. A plastic skirt in blue, white, pink, or red or a combination of these colors can be attached just ahead of the bait so that it rides draped over the bait's head and upper body. Or, even better, use a ⅛ oz-¼ oz Sea Witch in blue and white, pink and blue, red and black, or blue and gray; dark colors are for early morning, dusk, and overcast days and bright colors are for sunny days. Trim the strands of nylon in the front of the Sea Witch to 3" or 4" and use it like a plastic skirt, just ahead of the bait.

Ballyhoo: Fresh and frozen can be bought in bait and tackle stores or, as explained elsewhere, they can be caught. Use medium-size ballyhoo and a hook, leader, and skirt as for mullet.

Strip bait: A very effective bait because they fold so naturally in a sailfish's mouth, strips can be made from nearly any fish caught but generally are cut from mullet. Bonito are excellent and strips should be cut from their white belly or bluish sides about 6"-8" long, 2" wide, and 1/8" thick, with bevelled edges. Also, dolphin belly and mackerel filets are superb. Use a hook, leader, and skirt as above.

Artificial Bait. Anglers after dolphin have always caught sailfish on Japanese feathers. But only recently has a concerted effort been made using artificials. As with fishing for marlin, more ocean can be covered trolling an artificial at a higher speed than is possible with rigged dead bait. Therefore, some success has followed. One of the better baits in use for several years is an artificial strip bait rigged like a natural strip or with the addition of a piece of copper ballyhoo-rigging wire to secure it. In addition, use Moldcraft Softheads, Arbogast Reto's Rigs, Boone's Airheads, and other similar lures. No final word is in on what color skirt to use; try them all. Size may be the most important factor— up to 5″ or 6″ is about right. Trolling speed is also important but there is little agreement on this, either. The best advice is to try each lure at different speeds until the right combination is found.

Trolling During a Cold Front. When sailfish are swimming south in schools with their tails sticking up out of the water, a somewhat different technique is used. Find tailing fish and position the boat to travel just ahead of the fish. Let a rigged ballyhoo or mullet drop back to inside the fish's field of vision. Since the wind will be blowing from the north or northeast for the best of this kind of fishing, a lead egg-shaped weight up to 1 oz at the bait's head will keep it from flopping around in the seas. Also, #3 or #4 leader wire or 30# mono gives the bait a more life-like look and although a bit light, more action will result.

Balling Bait Fish. Sometimes sailfish will corral bait fish into a ball and, swimming around them, charge in, striking with their bills, in an attempt to put together a feast. This often occurs in the Stuart area but has recently been seen as far north as the mouth of the St. Johns River near Jacksonville. To catch sailfish while they are balling bait, back the boat up to the ball of bait and feeding sails and throw a rigged bait, alive or dead, to the nearest fish and jig rapidly. Often fish can be hooked so close in to the boat that only the leader is out of the rod tip.

Ocean Live-Baiting

From Jupiter south there is a greater concentration of sailfish than you will find in the water to the north. Consequently, covering a lot of water while fishing is not important and live-baiting is the preferred method. In waters to the north where fish are more scattered, a greater amount of ocean can be covered by trolling more rapidly with dead baits. (See section on live bait for instructions on how to catch and rig them, p. 154.) Southeast Florida sailfishermen rate the goggle eye as the best live bait.

Using a Kite. Special fishing kites can be bought in tackle stores and are used while the boat drifts, is anchored, or motors slowly. They are square-shaped and come in several sizes for use in various wind conditions. Kites have the advantage of keeping live bait away from the boat which reduces noise near the bait, of being away from the disturbing wake of the boat if moving, and of dangling the bait in the water so as to give it a natural look. The kite itself is attached to 50# Dacron which is best stored on a large fishing reel, about 9/0, and all of this is worked from a short fishing rod. After the kite is in the air 50' or more, clip the fishing line to the Dacron kite line, hook the live bait just ahead of the dorsal fin (above the backbone, not through it), and throw it out into the water. Fly the kite farther out so the bait ends up 75' to 100' from the boat. Set the reel on free spool with the click engaged so the line will not run out from wind or boat move-ment. When a sailfish takes the bait, it pulls free from the clip on the kite line. As usual, a leader must be used: 6'-8' 60#-80# mono. While kite-fishing, a deep-jigged strip bait will find fish if they are not at the surface. Attach the bait to a 1 oz or 2 oz white jig and work it down to the bottom.

Drift Fishing. Although one can sailfish from an anchored boat, drifting is superior for no other reason than you can cover various depths if the wind is blowing the right way. There is little danger of entangling lines because the boat will drift faster than the baits immersed in the water where there is greater resistance. But if the wind is not blowing as you like, you can troll very slowly. With the bait hooked as described in the rigging section of this book, lower it into the water and allow it to reach a predeter-mined distance as the boat moves away. Several baits can be fished at the same time: near and far, on the surface or deep (attach a 1 oz Rubbercor sinker to the leader below the swivel). If you want to keep the bait near the surface and also have a strike indicator, attach a balloon or a float to the swivel. The reel should be set as with kite fishing and the leader kept the same, as well. Still another method of live-baiting sailfish is using ballyhoo, pilchards, or pinfish on a downrigger. About 65' is the proper depth to send the bait and the boat must travel very slowly. During the summer in the "sailfish alley" section about 4 miles off the St. Johns River jetties, live menhaden are hooked through the nose and slow-trolled both at the surface and down to 15′ deep.

Keys Shallow Water Sailfishing. This is a special situation that capitalizes on the meeting of large schools of ballyhoo and sailfish, the result being a shower of bait in mid-air. Prepare tackle by doubling the fishing line for 3′ with a Bimini Twist and attach it, using a swivel, to 4′ of 50# mono or a length of leader sufficiently comfortable to cast. Attach a short-shank 4/0 copper-colored hook, and to its eye fasten a 6″ piece of copper rigging wire. Using a live ballyhoo, place the hook point inside the mouth and come down through the lower jaw. Lay the hook shank along the beak (with ballyhoo, the beak is on the lower jaw) and wrap the copper wire around the shank and beak and on out to the leader (a swivel in the leader at this point is useful to secure the end of the copper wire). Baits at this stage can be left in the live bait well until used. Cruise around looking for sailfish while scattering ballyhoo and cast the rigged live bait just ahead of a sighted fish. The spinning or plugging tackle described is sporty for this kind of fishing.

Fishing Piers. Use a live goggle eye and hook it on a bronze 6/0, attach a 50# leader about 8′ long, and tie a balloon on the connecting swivel. Float it out from the end of a pier on a west wind and if it's not a sail you catch, it will be something else equally exciting.

Fly Fishing

Use a leader with no butt section, only 6′ of 20# mono doubled at both ends with Bimini Twists and 1′ of a class tippet. Add 1′ of 80# mono as a shock tippet. The basic technique is to lure a sailfish using conventional but hookless baits, either live or dead, as teasers. When a fish is raised, it must be coaxed close enough to the boat to cast a fly and this is done by allowing it to mouth the bait and then pulling it out of the sail's mouth. When the fish is teased close enough, three things should happen at roughly the same time: the teaser should be pulled in completely; the boat should be stopped; and the fly cast to the fish. When the fish grabs the fly and turns, strike by pointing the rod at the fish and with the other hand sharply pull the line back two or three times. The telling is easier than the doing, but many fine sailfish have been caught this way. It is not for the lone fisherman: at least three people are necessary for this maneuver. Regarding which flies to use, two types are considered best: a 8"-12" streamer such as Lefty's Deceiver, with eyes, in white and with or without added red, blue, or green and with two 4/0-7/0 hooks lashed together and set at opposite angles; and the BM Fly. The second type is a large Gallasch-type popping bug in white with some red and tied on one hook, 3/0-7/0.

How to Hook a Sailfish

Using a kite: When a sailfish hits a kite-flown bait and the line drops out of the pin, there will be so much slack that the angler must first reel in as fast as he can. When the weight of the fish can be felt, strike at least twice.

Without a kite: Much has been written about the art of the "dropback" and a lot of it is nonsense. Because a sailfish is slow to take the hook as it turns the bait around in its mouth, some time must be allowed before setting the hook; this is true whether live- or dead-bait fishing. The best way to handle the problem is by keeping your eyes glued to the baits so that you are prepared. When a sail comes up on a bait—frequently turning neon blue in the process—the angler must get ready to feed line to it. This means that if the outrigger bait is pulled out of its pin, you must free-spool line to the fish; to apply tension at this point would flush the sailfish. Keep the thumb lightly on the turning spool so a tangle does not occur. As the speed picks up considerably, it means the sail is moving off with the bait. Throw the reel in gear (the drag of which has been set earlier to about 1/3 of the line's breaking strength), wait a second or two for slack to come out of the line, and set up on the hook. With a hit on a flat line, you don't have as much time to do all this as with an outrigger bait, but the same procedure must be followed. You can gain a second or two by attaching a short tag line to the flat line, a 2' or 3' clothesline that attaches to a stern cleat at one end and by means of a clothespin to the fishing line at the other.

If, after following these directions, you recognize there is no fish on the end of the line to strike, with the reel in gear, wind in line rapidly while holding the rod tip high in the air. When the bait is close enough to see, throw the reel out of gear and with your thumb again on the spool, you may get another chance at a fish doubling back. Fighting a well-hooked sail is a matter of lifting and lowering the rod tip, collecting line only on the lowering and so slowly that you put no slack into it. "Bow" to a jumping or tail-walking fish, or drop the rod tip and point it at the fish so as to reduce pressure on the line. On long runs, reduce the drag tension and then tighten up again when the fish settles down. Never tighten the tension more than 1/3 of the line's breaking strength.

How to Land a Sailfish. People have been seriously injured by the thrashing and jabbing bill of a sailfish, so it is wise to follow a certain landing procedure. First, make certain that the fish is no longer "green" but is truly exhausted. Head the boat downwind to increase steadiness. Station your fishing partner or mate toward the stern of the boat to one side or the other but not at the transom. When he can "wire" the fish, that is, grab hold of the leader with hands protected by wet cotton gloves, the boat handler should speed up just enough so that the mate can raise the fish's head while the tail skims over the water.

The idea is to have just enough speed on so that the sailfish cannot dip its powerful tail in the water to find purchase for a lunge. With the fish in this position, the mate grabs the bill (never with thumb around bill) and slides the fish into the fish box. At this point, bending the fish head towards tail subdues it, enabling one to hold it down with just one hand. Now a properly placed blow on the head just behind the eyes with a billy club should end the fight. To release a sailfish (always recommended), while the fish is in the water hold the bill and clip the leader as close as possible to the hook. If the fish is exhausted and needs reviving, hold it upright in the water while the boat moves slowly ahead. Note one important point: Never, never gaff a sailfish as it could possibly result in someone being injured by the thrashing fish.

Other Fish Caught While Fishing for Sailfish. Dolphin, tunas, wahoo, kingfish, white marlin, and, very occasionally, a blue marlin.

Regulations

- Closed Season: none
- Minimum Size: 57" tip of lower jaw to fork in tail
- Maximum Size: no regulation
- Daily Bag Limit: one per day of any billfish

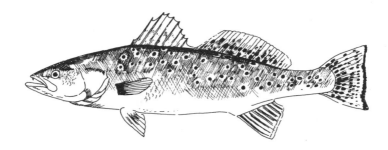

22

Spotted Seatrout; Trout; Speckled Trout
(Cynoscion nebulosus)

Perhaps one of the most sought-after fishes in Florida, trout are not only good fighters, especially on light tackle, but they make a delicious dinner, too. The spotted seatrout occurs over nearly the entire coast of the state and therefore is the most important member of its group of look-alikes: weakfish (*Cynoscion regalis*); the uncommon sand seatrout (*Cynoscion arenarius*); and the silver seatrout (*Cynoscion nothus*). An angler can expect to find them as follows:

- Spotted seatrout: entire Florida coast except from Boynton to Miami and the Lower Keys.
- Weakfish: Indian River north.
- Sand seatrout: Naples north.
- Silver seatrout: Indian River north and the Panhandle.

Most of the following information refers to the spotted seatrout, but the other varieties will be caught on occasion. Preferred water temperature: 65°–75° F. All-tackle record: 17 lb 7 oz.

WHERE AND WHEN

1. Indian and Banana rivers area (from the tip of Merritt
    Island to the St. Lucie Inlet at Stuart). Known as the part of
    Florida where the largest trout are taken, this stretch has
    literally thousands of places that offer excellent fishing, all
    of it inside and protected from the open ocean by long
    barrier islands. Trout like warm water and dislike cold, so
    expect to find them in warm weather in the shallow water
    covering grass flats and spoil islands and when cold, in
    deep water channels, dropoffs, and residential canals. Dur-
    ing the winter around mid-day or after if the water warms
    enough, trout can also be found in the shallows. Normally,
    trout are surface-feeding from about March to October and
    deep-feeding from November through February. Because
    they avoid rapid currents, trout are best fished during slack
    tides and on the first and last of the flood and ebb tides. As
    with most fishes, early and late in the day are the best times
    and an overcast is better than a sunny day. The day before
    an advancing cold front and two or three days afterwards
    are considered prime times. During the winter, power
    plant outfalls provide warm water and therefore a congre-
    gating place for seatrout. Some well-known fishing loca-
    tions in this region are the canals along the east side of the
    Indian River north of Sebastian Inlet; the east shore of the
    Indian River just south of Sebastian Inlet; the Crossroads at
    Stuart; the flats north of the Jungle Trail in Vero Beach; and
    so many more that it would be difficult to list them. Any
    local bait and tackle store is a good resource for information.
2. Biscayne Bay, the Upper Keys, and Southwest Florida. As in
    the preceding section, trout are caught here year-round
    but the fish are larger in the spring. While the first cold
    weather elsewhere in Florida drives seatrout into deep,
    warm water, in this region expect trout to move onto the
    grass flats. A continued cold spell, however, will cause
    trout to seek deep water. A good place to fish is a clear
    water basin about 3'-6' deep with some yellow grass and
    patches of sand and grass appearing light and dark green.
    The deeper the water, the larger the fish you'll catch. The
    high slack tide and the last flood and first ebb on either side

of it are considered the best times to fish. Some locations include in front of Mercy Hospital in Biscayne Bay down to Chicken Key on the mainland side; the large sounds in the Upper Keys such as Blackwater and Barnes; Madeira Bay between Key Largo and Flamingo in the Everglades National Park; and the flats off Cape Romano in the Ten Thousand Islands. Of course, there are many more excellent places in this vast, relatively untouched part of Florida.

3. Atlantic coast north of Titusville and the entire Gulf coast. This immense region covers most of Florida's coastline and there are thousands of good seatrout fishing places. Any bay or sound where there are grass flats mixed with sand patches giving a checkerboard look to the bottom is a good location; also seek out deeper cuts and holes as well as residential canals for winter fishing. A depth finder is useful to locate such places. Although seatrout rarely venture into the open ocean along the Atlantic coast, on the Gulf coast during the summer they can be found 10-15 miles out on grass flats that, even that far from shore, are only 10'-15' deep. These fish head for coastal rivers, passes, and creeks along the shore in cold weather and spend some time feeding on grass flats, sand ledges, and oyster bars as long as they are near deep, warm water. Later, with the onset of cold weather, seatrout move into warmer fresh water creeks and rivers. In October, along the Gulf coast in from 8'-10' of water, there is a shrimp migration and trout—as well as many other fishes—go into a feeding frenzy and stir up great clouds of mud; at such a time they can be caught with almost any bait. In most places on these two coastlines, the first hour or two of ebb tide is the right time to fish except for large harbors and bays where a half-in, half-out tide is right. Nighttime fishing from the shore is a productive method. Year-round fishing is the case along these two coasts with March known for the presence of "gator" trout, large fish over 6 lb. Some of the best times and places on the Atlantic coast are June through September in the Mosquito Lagoon east of Oak Hill and in November from Matanzas Inlet to Fernandina Beach. On the Gulf coast any time of the year at the large Charlotte Harbor estuary near Placida; the Crystal River and Homo-

sassa areas in mid-October and then again in the spring with April being tops; the Cedar Keys from September through December; and the Suwannee and Steinhatchee River mouths from the middle of November until the end of January.

4. Special mention of the weakfish (gray trout, squeteague) is necessary as it is an important sport fish in northeast Florida. In our area it doesn't grow as large as the spotted seatrout but is caught at the same time although usually in water 18′ deep and more. The inlet and the jetties of the St. Johns River are well-known for weakfish, especially from October to as late as May. Fish for it the same way as you would for the spotted seatrout.

TACKLE

Spinning and Plug Casting. Light tackle is the best approach for trout. A 7′ rod; 4#-8# line (a little heavier if not in open water), mono or braided; spin or conventional reel.

Fly. About a 8½′ 7 weight rod, heavier where it is deep and when it is windy; slow or fast-sinking, weight-forward line.

TECHNIQUES

Natural Bait

Live Bait

Shrimp: Probably the most commonly used bait for seatrout: the larger the shrimp, the better. The use of a leader will depend on where you are fishing: if it is open water, use none; if there are mangroves or other such places on which line can fray and break, use a 3′ mono leader twice as heavy as the fishing line and increase its size if that is not enough. Using an improved clinch knot, attach a bronze #4 or #6 treble hook (single #2 to 2/0 if record-qualifying is important) to the end of the leader or line and about 3′ above attach a popping cork. Thread a live shrimp on the hook. The rig should be kept light so the shrimp can move around easily but in order to keep it on the bottom where it must be to catch fish, you may need to add a 1/8 oz Rubbercor or #7 split shot lead about 6" above the hook. If fishing in a harbor, drift across, popping the cork loudly every few seconds. If fishing in a deep hole, a canal, or along mangroves, cast to the selected spot and pop the cork occasionally. Live shrimp can also be effectively fished by freelining. Hook a shrimp under the horn on its head and use no cork or swivel and preferably no leader as you allow the shrimp to work its way under mangroves or into other likely spots. If drifting, allow up to 100' of line to pay out to keep the shrimp down and deep. Large trout can be caught at night on shrimp especially during the spring. At the less-lighted part of a bridge near grass flats, lower a gas lantern that has foil over it to keep the light from your eyes. Tie it to something only 4' or so above the water and fish a live shrimp on light line. If the tide keeps the shrimp from sinking, attach an ounce or so of weight 2' above the bait.

Fish: See the section on live bait regarding how to catch and keep each species. The rig should be the same as for shrimp. Mullet are used all over the state; yellowtail (not the snapper) is an Indian River area choice; pigfish are considered tops in the Indian River and Mosquito Lagoon; pinfish are popular on the Gulf coast; and needle fish are used in various areas but especially the central Atlantic coast. When fishing with live bait, place a 1 oz egg sinker on the line above a swivel and attach 2' of 20# mono as a leader to effectively work passes or inlets when there is much current. Hook the live bait through the lips and drift with the tide, letting it roll along the bottom. Also, for good nighttime trout fishing, see the directions for fishing with shrimp at night and do the same with live fishes.

Dead Bait. Fished under a popping cork the same way as with live bait, dead fish parts are effective baits. Mullet strips about 2" long and ¼" wide and a split tail from a 3"-6" pinfish should be used with a 1/0-3/0 hook and kept deep in the water with 1/8 oz of lead, Rubbercor or #7 split shot, 6" above the bait. With this rig, drift by potholes and over grass and occasionally pop the cork loudly. Another method of preparing pinfish as bait is to make a diagonal cut from in front of the dorsal fin to the back of the anal fin, cutting the fish in half. Using only the portion with the tail, place the hook under the dorsal fin and fish it beneath a popping cork.

Artificial Bait

Spin and Plug Casting. Each part of Florida's seatrout country has its own favorite artificial bait. It may be that all catch fish everywhere, but it is wise to stick with what is locally used. Fish artificials in the same kind of water as you would natural bait: seek out the deep spots when it is cold and the shallows when it is warm. Sometimes when it begins to cool during November on the upper Gulf coast, trout can be caught as they move over the shallows to reach creeks and rivers.

1. Indian River area and north: In deep water allow sinking lures to go to the bottom and retrieve slowly with upward twitches of the rod tip. Surface lures also should be retrieved slowly, partly swimming and partly twitched along. Lures good for deep water are the grubtail jig; the Sassy Shad with a yellow or red head and a fluorescent, clear, or white tail, with or without a tiny piece of shrimp on the hook; the Cotee Swimming Glitter Shad with a tail the color of motor oil, root beer, purple, or chartreuse; a ¼ oz gold Johnson spoon; the Mirrolure 52M and TT series with a green or black back, white belly, and silver scales; the Boone Needlefish; and a lead-head jig with no tail but a live shrimp, instead, and fished as with a jig by bouncing it slowly along the bottom. Shallow-water lures are the Mirrolure 7M series with a dark back; the Bagley Finger Mullet; the Rebel Jumpin' Minnow; all the Zara types; and a small Rapala with hooks replaced by the stronger, salt water type.
2. Everglades area to the Upper Keys: Follow the same directions as in the preceding section regarding lure retrieval. Use these artificials: a ¼ oz silver Johnson spoon with a 2″ plastic worm in pink or red; a red head and white body tout; a ¼ oz yellow bucktail; a Creek Chub Darter; a Burke Top-Dog; and floating or sinking Mirrolures in 7M and 52M series in green and white or red and white in clear water and chartreuse in dirty water.

3. Charlotte Harbor area: Use the Sassy Shad; the Bagley Chug-O-Lure; and the Bomber Rip Shad with a red head and white belly. An infrequently seen but highly effective lure in southwest Florida is a noisy chugging plug connected to a 1/8 oz lead-head jig trailing about 2' behind. A short piece of wooden dowel or broom handle can be fashioned into the plug part. Fish it by retrieving a few feet and stopping to allow the jig to sink, and retrieving again.

4. Central and northern Gulf coast: Use a mirror-sided plug; a ¼ oz grubtail jig with a red or black head and a tail colored motor oil or pink glitter and tip with shrimp; a Zara Spook with an attached ¼ oz grubtail jig a foot or so behind, and fish it as above, pausing between retrieves; a Cordell Crazy Shad especially at night; and a ¼ oz silver Johnson spoon. While standing on the shore of a pass or creek, cast a jig or trout tout about 3 o'clock on the downcurrent side, let it settle to the bottom, and raise and lower the rod tip so the lure moves up and down over the bottom until the line is taut and it is downcurrent of you. Reel in and repeat.

Fly. Seatrout offer excellent fishing for the wading fly fisherman as miles of grass flats are available, as indicated above. For surface fishing make about a 10'-12' leader: 4' 25#, 3' 20#, 2' 15#, 1' 12#, and a 1' 8# or 10# tippet. A 10" piece of 30# shock can be added if other fish cut the leader. For large flies reduce the overall length to 7½' and in deep water with a sinking line, a 4' leader will do. On grassy flats use a weedless surface fly; if it is overcast, keep the color dark but use bright colors if it is sunny. Fish flies by stripping 10" of line at a time. Use Seaducers and Deceivers in all white, all yellow, blue and white, red and yellow, red and white, all black, grizzly and yellow; flies with fluorescent colors; needle fish imitations; a Chico's Bend Back in orange and yellow, 1/0-3/0 hook; a Dahlberg Diver in white; a glass minnow in green and white, 3"-4"; a Dave's Salt Shrimp; and bugs made by Gaines, Arbogast, and Accardo.

How to Hook a Seatrout. Seatrout hit hard and the tendency is to set the hook with force. But don't, since they have a mouth that tears easily; set softly and don't try to "horse" them in.

Other Fish Caught While Fishing for Seatrout. Jack crevalle, redfish, snook, Spanish mackerel, bluefish, and ladyfish.

Regulations

- Closed Season: NW Florida, February; Flagler County north, December through February; remainder of state, November and December
- Minimum Size: 15″ overall
- Maximum Size: 20″ overall
- Daily Bag Limit: 7 in NW Florida; 5 in rest of the state (one fish anywhere in the state may be longer than 24″)
- Note: Seatrout must be brought in with head and fins intact.
- Note: There are no regulations for the other trouts mentioned.

23

Sharks

A diverse group of powerful ocean creatures, some sharks require rope to haul in, others, when hooked, leap to 30′, and still others can be taken on a fly rod. Sharks have in the last few years been recognized for their great sport potential. The following are the common Florida species for which the International Game Fish Association keeps all-tackle records:

- Hammerhead shark (*Sphyrna spp.*) 991 lb
- Tiger shark (*Galeocerdo cuvieri*) 1,780 lb
- Sand tiger shark (*Odontaspis taurus*) 350 lb 2 oz
- Lemon shark (*Negaprion brevirostris*) 405 lb
- Mako shark (*Isurus oxyrinchus*) 1,115 lb
- Blacktip shark (*Carcharhinus limbatus*) 270 lb 9 oz
- Spinner shark (*Carcharhinus brevipinna*) 190 lb
- Dusky or sand shark (*Carcharhinus obscurus*) 764 lb
- Bull shark (*Carcharhinus leucas*) 490 lb
- Sandbar or brown shark (*Carcharhinus plumbeus*) 260 lb
- Blacknose shark (*Carcharhinus acronotus*) 41 lb 9 oz

The IGFA keeps no records for:

- Nurse shark (*Ginglymostoma cirratum*)
- Bonnethead shark (*Sphyrna tiburo*)
- Silky shark (*Carcharhinus falciformis*)

These sharks are rarely eaten although the hammerhead and mako are considered fair food. Preferred water temperature is the seventies.

WHERE AND WHEN

Sharks of one kind or another are in Florida's saltwaters all year and are especially active at certain times. For example, July is a good month for spinner and blacktip sharks because then they are close to shore on both coasts of south Florida and the Keys, but they also bite all spring and summer. Hammerheads are active in the fall and during the winter can be found on the surface of the Gulf Stream and inshore water. Bull sharks are present in Charlotte Harbor in July and Key West in March. Deep water at the Bahia Honda bridge in the Keys produces large sharks almost the entire year.

During warm weather, sharks are in the shallow waters of the surf, bays, and inlets but if it becomes too hot, they retreat to deeper, cooler water. On the same note, to avoid cold winters more sharks are found in the southern part of the state, but when it is warm they can be caught up and down both coasts. In shallow water where sight casting for sharks is possible, look for them early and late in the day during summer, and try the first few hours of dark, as well.

TACKLE

Deep Water. Bridge fishing for large sharks calls for heavy equipment in order to control the creatures: a 130# outfit. A 6′ glass rod and a conventional reel holding at least 300 yd of Dacron line is about right. Open water fishing such as offshore in a boat is pursued with as little as a 25# or as much as an 80# outfit with other equipment as above.

Spinning and Plug Casting. Although a shark weighing more than 414 lb was caught on 12# class line, to repeat this phenomenon is not a realistic goal. Sharks to 3′ or so can be caught on 4#-6# gear while those around 50 lb can be handled on a 15# outfit. Rods about 6′ long and reels holding at least 200 yd of line, mono or braided, are required. Use a 10′ surf spinning rod, about a 20# outfit, to enable you to get out beyond the waves.

Fly. On the flats, use a 7-9 weight rod and floating line to match and a reel holding at least 200 yd of Dacron backing. For big sharks in deep water when larger flies may be needed, use equipment as described under Sailfish, p. 84 plus a fast sinking line.

TECHNIQUES

Deep Water. Whether offshore on the Atlantic coast at the 100 fathom line or fishing deep water swirling around a bridge, the use of fishes, either live or dead, is the best way to catch sharks. The gamest of them all, the leaping mako—as well as the tiger and hammerhead—responds to belly-rigged mackerel, mullet, or strips from bonito or blackfin tuna. For this kind of trolling for very large fish, you'll need a 15' leader made of cable, #15 wire, or 300# mono plus extra-strong hooks, size 10/0-14/0. For smaller fish around 100 lb, 3' or 4' of #7 wire plus 5' or 6' of 80#-100# mono will be fine. If you see a large shark on the surface—not an uncommon sight—maneuver the boat so the bait crosses the animal's field of vision on one side of its head or the other.

In the fall in south Florida you can drift in 100'-300' of water and fish a 3-lb dead bonito deep for sandbar sharks and fish another bait or two at different levels maintained by floats. At the same time you can try the surface on a flat line or a kite (see Sailfish section, p. 88) for hammerheads. Live blue runners or nearly any other small live fish would work; good dead bait are ballyhoo and barracuda, the latter having an odor that is specially attractive to sharks. Of course, chum motivates sharks, especially when it is very oily or bloody. Menhaden chum can be bought in frozen chunks and is very oily; for bloody chum you will need to catch your own and bonito are excellent. Some fishermen get blood from animal slaughter houses to use mixed with solid fish chum. Barracuda, as previously indicated, because of their particular odor, make fine chum. Once sharks get the scent and come up to the boat, fish for them as previously described.

Shallow Water

Natural bait: The technique of using bait as previously mentioned works in the shallows, too. If you fish from the shore, you can catch sharks if you position yourself properly. In the surf along the Atlantic coast, spinner and blacktip sharks are best caught with a live mullet hooked between the dorsal and tail fins and cast out beyond the waves. As long a leader as possible, one that still makes casting comfortable, is necessary; wire testing 100#-120# or mono 150#-200# is alright. Hooks are about 9/0. An inlet, bridge, a channel edge where the tide runs swiftly, or where a river and a bay join are all good locations. The best place is where the current will carry the odor of your chum to deeper water nearby. In protected water of these types, mullet and ladyfish make excellent dead bait while live pinfish and whatever else you can catch are productive if freelined in the current.

Artificial bait: Casting for sharks is really good sport and the fight can test anyone's fishing ability. Blacktip sharks are regarded as very willing to hit artificials and others, such as the lemon, bull, nurse, and small hammerheads can be taken, too. On light equipment, 1′ of #3 or #4 wire should be attached to the lure and as much 30# mono added to allow casting. Use no swivels; attach the mono to the line with a double surgeon's knot and to the wire with an Albright Special. Noisy surface plugs and sub-surface darter types are the best.

Fly Fishing for Sharks. You may not come near to the record of a shark over 114 lb, on an 8# tippet, but you will catch them on a fly rod, as out of place as such a pursuit seems. In deep water, chum as previously explained. When the sharks come up, cast, using a 3″-5″ weighted streamer in red and yellow or blue and white tied on a 5/0 hook; retrieve slowly. For this kind of fishing when the sharks may be quite large, use a leader whose butt is 50# and together with the tippet measures 7′ or 8′ long; a 1′ piece of #5 wire as a shock should be attached to the mono with an Albright Special knot. For smaller sharks in shallow water, the same length leader is made from 30# for the butt, and the shock can be made from #3 wire or 50# or 60# mono. Use streamers 2″-3″, poppers, sliders, or a muddler in white and red on about a 3/0 hook. Fish the flood tide and chum if sharks are not cruising. Cast and work the fly in such a way that the shark will see it for the longest possible time. It is necessary to set the hook hard on a shark; read the section on tarpon concerning the correct method, p. 138.

How to Land a Shark. Large sharks should never be boated no matter how dead you think they are. There are too many instances of "dead" sharks coming to life in the cockpit. Consider how you might handle such a situation with several hundred pounds of biting and thrashing shark. Use a flying gaff (see the Blue Marlin section, p. 64) and leave them in the water; if you intend to take a shark back to the dock, lash it alongside the boat. Use a conventional gaff on smaller sharks. However, sharks are no different from all the fishes discussed in this book: they should be released unless you intend to eat them. Few people like the idea of eating shark and one hanging wasted on a meat hook is one that will never again follow your chum line to crash a bait.

Other Fish Caught While Fishing for Sharks. In deep water when you are trolling, dolphin, marlin, and wahoo—in shallow water, bluefish, snook, trout, ladyfish, and tarpon.

Regulations

- Closed Season: none
- Minimum Size: no regulation
- Maximum Size: no regulation
- Daily Bag Limit: 1 per person or 2 per boat, whichever is less

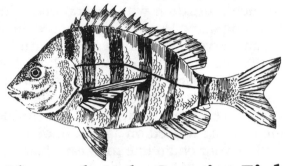

24

Sheepshead; Convict Fish
(*Archosargus probatocephalus*)

A real challenge to catch as it is such a clever bait thief, the sheepshead is a popular fish caught in nearly every part of the state. They are excellent to eat. All-tackle record: 21 lb 4 oz.

WHERE AND WHEN

1. Southern part of the state, particularly along inshore reefs and inside inlets from Palm Beach to Melbourne, and in the deep channels and along mangroves in the Ten Thousand Islands, Everglades National Park, and on up the Gulf coast to the Charlotte Harbor area where the fishing is superb. Sheepshead are caught all year but fall and winter are best, especially when it is cold; March is a peak time on the Gulf coast. Slack and ebb tides are the best times to fish.
2. Northern part of the state, particularly near navigation markers, pilings, and rocks on the Gulf coast and inlet jetties on the northeast part of the coastline. Winter is the best time of the year and the ebb and slack tides are the times to fish. The largest sheepshead are caught in this region.

TACKLE

Spinning and Plug Casting. For smaller fish, use a 5'-7' medium-heavy rod, while larger fish require a boat rod with considerable beef; 15#-20# line (heavier if near structure), mono or braided; spin or conventional reel.

TECHNIQUES

Natural Bait. Live or dead shrimp, sand fleas, fiddler crabs, pieces of larger crabs, tube worms, and clams are all good sheepshead bait. The kind of bait used depends on what is locally available but, whatever it is, try to bury the hook in it. A good technique is to pinch off the tail flippers of a live shrimp and thread it on the hook. Buy or catch fiddler crabs on mud flats at low tide in warm weather. Rig by breaking off the large claw of the male fiddler and placing a short-shank 2/0 hook in the crab at the base of the second leg from the rear and pushing until the point reaches but does not penetrate the top shell. The most important part of fishing for sheepshead is chum, and some effort should be made to obtain it. Any of the preceding baits ground up fine would be alright, but rather expensive. It is cheaper to use barnacles scraped off pilings of a bridge or fresh oyster shells from an oyster bar. Crush and pulverize these with a hammer and cast them into the water upcurrent of any kind of structure: jetties, pilings, markers, wrecks, docks, seawalls, etc. In the Everglades area, find oyster bars and deep holes and channels; hard bottoms with clean, white sand are preferred. In the open ocean, fish the deep sloughs in the surf and inshore reefs that are close to shore. Use a pinch-on weight or a sliding sinker rig with a ½ oz egg sinker; go heavier if there is current as it is necessary to keep the bait close to or on the bottom whether the fish are in 3' or 30' of water. But because sheepshead are notorious bait stealers, the less weight you use the more you will be sensitive to a fish trying to steal your bait. A sliding sinker rig should be constructed so that the sinker is on 12" of shock leader, about 20#-30# mono, which is attached to the line with a swivel. With shrimp use a #1 or 1/0 hook or, if the fish run large as they do in the winter off

Cedar Keys, go up to 3/0 or 4/0. Keep it extremely sharp to pierce the tough mouth of a sheepshead. Shrimp can be cast, particularly over hard bottoms such as oyster bars, and slowly jigged for the retrieve or you can fish on the bottom giving the bait little or no motion.

Artificial Bait. A shrimp-tipped jig can be cast out and worked back slowly in the same locations as above. However, the real value of this bait is the weight, which makes casting easier. Many fishermen cut away the nylon or feathers of a jig and thread a live shrimp on the hook; or they just buy a bare jig head and bait it with a shrimp. This is especially effective if you want to fish deep in a hole or channel.

How to Hook a Sheepshead. For a practiced bait thief such as this fish, some care must be taken to get a solid hook-up. Allow a sheepshead to nibble at the bait but don't react, as it would flush the fish. As it moves off with the bait you will feel a sudden change to something heavy on the end of the line. That is the time to set the hook by striking hard, really with a force just under the breaking strength of the line used. If there is good hook penetration, there will be no problem landing the fish with or without a net.

Other Fish Caught While Fishing for Sheepshead. Snappers, pompano, spotted seatrout, redfish, and snook.

Regulations

- Closed Season: none
- Minimum Size: 12″ from nose to fork in tail
- Maximum Size: no regulation
- Daily Bag Limit: 15

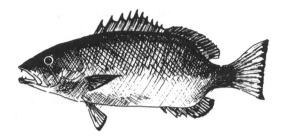

25

Snappers

For their accessibility in nearly all of Florida's saltwater and for their excellent sport fishing, if a vote were taken, snappers would probably win over all other fishes. The Florida species for which the International Game Fish Associaton keeps all-tackle records are the following:

- Cubera snapper (*Lutjanus cyanopterus*) 121 lb 8 oz, found in south Florida on rocky ledges in water 60'–200' deep.
- Gray or mangrove snapper (*Lutjanus griseus*) 17 lb, found all around Florida from inshore waters a few feet deep to offshore in 300' of water.
- Lane snapper (*Lutjanus synagris*) 7 lb, found all around Florida from coral reefs to inshore brackish water.
- Mutton snapper (*Lutjanus analis*) 28 lb 5 oz, found all around Florida from the shallow water of Keys' flats out to the ocean reef.
- Red snapper (*Lutjanus campechanus*) 50 lb 4 oz, found in water 150'–300' deep.
- Silk snapper (*Lutjanus vivanus*) 18 lb 5 oz, found all around Florida in water 300'–800' deep.
- Yellowtail snapper (*Ocyurus chrysurus*) 8 lb 9 oz, found all around Florida but especially in the southern part in water 60'–300' deep.

Other common snappers for which the IGFA keeps no records are the schoolmaster (*Lutjanus apodus*) which reaches about two feet; the dog snapper (*Lutjanus jocu*) which reaches three feet; the mahogany snapper (*Lutjanus mahogoni*) which reaches one foot; the blackfin snapper (*Lutjanus buccanella*) which reaches 30 lb; the queen snapper (*Etelis oculatus*) which reaches three feet; and the vermilion snapper (*Rhomboplites aurorubens*) which reaches 6 lb. The red snapper, a deep-water fish, prefers a temperature of 57°-60° F. while the others like 66°-86° F. The best to eat are the red, mutton, yellowtail, gray, and lane snappers; very large snappers may have ciguatera poisoning, which is dangerous to humans.

WHERE AND WHEN

Some snappers are caught all year all over the state from shallow water inside passes and bays to offshore out to 25 miles or more on the Gulf coast. As with groupers, snappers prefer bottom structure and nearly always are found around rocks, wrecks, patch and offshore reefs, bridges, docks, etc. There are published lists of both compass and Loran coordinates of known excellent bottom locations and these can be purchased by mail or in bait and tackle stores. Some well-known places and times for snapper fishing are the Key West flats in the spring and fall for muttons; Atlantic reefs in 35'-50' of water in June and July for grays, especially at night when the moon is full; the Panhandle for red snapper in 240' of water or so in the fall; off the northeast coast beginning about April; and on the Atlantic side of the Keys and southeast Florida in late spring and early summer in 60'-120' of water.

TACKLE

Bottom Fishing. For small snapper such as the gray and lane, any light spinning or bait casting rod to handle 8#-15# line, mono or braided; for large snapper such as mutton and cubera, a 50#-80# outfit with a stout 5½' glass stand-up rod; Dacron line; conventional 4/0 reel.

Flats Fishing. For mutton snapper, follow the tackle recommendations for permit, p. 70, and use fly, spinning, or plug casting equipment.

TECHNIQUES

Bottom Fishing

Over 300′ of Water. Fishing in such deep water is best left to commercial fishermen, but heavy rigs fished off ledges, wrecks, reefs, and other such structure as described for grouper can be productive. Wire line and/or heavy weights are used to get to the bottom and electric reels make sense for the long haul back up. Use cut squid, cigar minnows, or large live fishes as bait. For large red snapper, use whole squids, whole 2-3 lb fish, and bloody pieces of bonito.

Up to 200′ of Water

Cubera: On reefs in the southeast and the Keys, especially around Careysfort whistle buoy, spawning time about one week before the August full moon is best. These large fish are best caught at night in 120′-200′ of water and heavy grouper tackle is necessary. The best bait is live Florida lobster (saltwater crawfish). Use a double hook rig, each 9/0 or larger, connected by wire several inches apart, depending on the size of the lobster. The first hook should be passed between the "horns" of the crustacean to come out on the underside. The end hook should be passed into the soft tail on the underneath side and out the very tip end of the animal. Small live fishes such as grunt, yellowtail, and blue runners hooked through the back, in front of the dorsal fin are good but definitely second-best to Florida lobster. Many of the techniques used for deep fishing for grouper are effective with snapper so that section of this book should be read (p. 35).

Mutton: On the outer reefs in 90′-150′ of water and from the central Atlantic coast through the Keys, mutton snapper are caught in the winter and mid-summer. Live ballyhoo hooked through the upper jaw with a 5/0 short shank hook should be

combined with 3'-4' of 80# mono as a leader; add enough lead
to get to the bottom. Live pilchards are also very effective if
hooked through the anal fin with the point coming out
through the ventral fin. At least 50# line is necessary to yank a
hooked fish away from the reef. Lower the bait and when the
weight hits bottom take ten to fifteen turns of the reel handle
to raise it away from bottom-hugging groupers. One can also
troll deep for mutton with a dead ballyhoo rigged on a 2-oz
feather jig or a tube lure, the same kind used for barracuda.

Gray (called mangrove snapper, usually, but in the Panhandle,
black snapper): Although grays can be caught well inshore,
especially during cold weather, and in the same places where
redfish and trout are found, to meet the minimum-size regulations currently in force, one may have to fish the reefs and on
the lower Gulf coast as far as 25 miles offshore. At any rate, gray
snapper can be found in 8'-12' of water in such places as off
docks, light sand patches in a grassy bottom, holes and ledges
in passes and coastal rivers, and nearly anywhere that mangrove trees are growing. Full moon, nighttime fishing in
summer, when grays spawn is considered prime time. If fishing
from a boat, always anchor upcurrent of whatever bottom
structure you intend to explore; 40'-50' away is not too far.
No matter where you try, using chum is the most successful
approach.

Chum should be released so that it floats down upon the
chosen spot, or, if in deep water, the bag or chum container
should be weighted to go to the bottom. Start with a medium-
sized outfit such as 12#-15# plus a 30# mono leader a foot or
two long. If the fish refuse to bite, first eliminate the leader, and
if that doesn't get things going, drop down in line size to 8# or
10#. A 1/0-2/0 short shank hook is about right and bait can be
live shrimp—a mangrove favorite—or cut mullet, squid, a
pinfish "steak", or cigar minnows; for large grays try small, live
fish. Egg sinkers from ¼-1 oz placed above the swivel or knot
attaching the leader are only necessary in current and should
be only heavy enough to get the bait down to the fish. Lower
the baited line and raise just off the bottom after the weight
hits. A guppy rig can be used; its multiple baits give you extra
shots at the fish. Artificials such as 1/8-oz or 1/16-oz jigs with a
grubtail attached or tipped with a piece of shrimp are good if

they are allowed to sink to the bottom and then retrieved rapidly. Sometimes mangrove snappers hit surface plugs around 4″ long when one fishes for snook in shallow water.

Lane: Because keepers start at only 8″ long, lanes are a good substitute for grays, are equally good to eat, and are found in the same places. Use the same techniques and equipment as described for grays.

Yellowtail: Large yellowtail or "flags" are among the trickiest of snappers to catch but, because they are such good food, it is very worthwhile to give it your best attempt. Although they can be caught over reefs elsewhere in Florida, the Keys are undoubtedly the best location. On the outer reef margin and over a shelf in about 100′ of water in the late spring and early summer is the time and place to be; as it gets warmer as in August, you must fish a little deeper and during the night. Yellowtail can be caught anytime, however, and during the winter the first two or three days after a cold front has passed through is a good time to try. Tackle can be the same as for grays but yellowtail are even more wary of heavy line; use leaders only at nighttime and the lightest test line possible to still bring in fish. Weighted chum bags are necessary and a few glass minnows thrown into the water every few minutes will help bring the yellowtail up.

Bait can be the same as for grays, but some fishermen fillet ballyhoo and trim each fillet into three strips. Coat the flesh side of the strips with coarse salt and store on crushed ice. Thread a ballyhoo strip on a bronze #2 hook and, with whatever bait used, with the reel in free spool allow it to drift back to chummed-up yellowtail. When a fish grabs the bait, give it a second or two and set the hook. If the fish remain deep, use enough lead to get the bait down to them, about 1/8 oz to ½ oz with the egg sinker attached about 3′ above the hook. In heavy current and at night, up to 3 oz of lead can be used.

Jigging. See the jigging instructions in the chapter on grouper (p. 37) and jig deep for snapper in the same way.

Flats Fishing. Catching mutton snapper on the flats is considered as much of a challenge as bonefish and permit — and it may even be harder to do. Unquestionably, a flood tide on the ocean side flats from Key West to the Marquesas Keys during March and April and then again in September and October are the hottest areas and times. Bayside flats in the Keys are fished on the ebb tide but are definitely second best. Muttons are hunted and then sight-fished and fishermen look for the pink to red sides of tailing fish or for such fish signs as sand and mud trails left by rays and sharks; cormorants circling over flats often are above fish. And just like tailing bonefish, muttons are after small creatures stirred up in the sand. A 4″ wide crab is the best bait and it should be fished as described for permit (p. 70); live shrimp can be used, too. Because fishes on flats are usually easy to flush, cast no closer than 10′ to a sighted fish. Fly rod artificials can be the epoxy fly, crab and shrimp imitations, small fish imitations such as of a mullet, and, in general, those flies ordinarily used on redfish and tarpon. Retrieve in 3″-4″ strips.

How to Land a Snapper. It is common in snapper fishing to lose bait because the fisherman strikes too soon. Allow the fish to run a few seconds while you free spool the line; then set hard. Also, not reacting to small fish nibbling at the bait will allow the keepers to move in for a mouthful.

Other Fish Caught While Fishing for Snappers. On the reef expect grouper, amberjack, barracuda, kingfish, and, when using a live fish as bait, sailfish. On the flats expect bonefish and permit.

Regulations

- Closed Season: none
- Gray: Minimum Size: 10″ overall
    Maximum Size: no regulation
    Daily Bag Limit: 5
- Red: Minimum Size: Gulf, 16″ overall; Atlantic, 20″ overall
    Maximum Size: no regulation
    Daily Bag Limit: Gulf, 5; Atlantic, 2
- Schoolmaster: Minimum Size: 10″ overall
        Maximum Size: no regulation
        Daily Bag Limit: 10

- Mutton: Minimum Size: 16″ overall
    Maximum Size: no regulation
    Daily Bag Limit: 10
- Cubera: Minimum Size: 12″ overall
    Maximum Size: no regulation
    Daily Bag Limit: no more than 2 fish 30″ or longer
- Yellowtail, queen, mahogany, silk, and blackfin:
    Minimum Size: 12″ overall
    Maximum Size: no regulation
    Daily Bag Limit: 10
- Lane: Minimum Size: 8″ overall
    Maximum Size: no regulation
    Daily Bag Limit: no regulation
- Vermilion: Minimum Size: Gulf and Atlantic, 10″ overall
    Maximum Size: no regulation
    Daily Bag Limit: Gulf, no regulation; Atlantic, 10
- Note: The 10 daily limit means that each day a fisherman may catch 10 snappers of various kinds (with the exception of grays and reds which are limited as described). Lane and Gulf vermilion are exempt. All snappers must be brought in with head and fins intact.

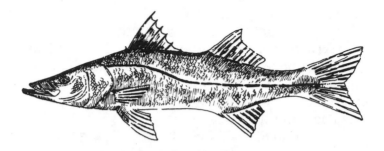

26

Snook; Robalo; Saltwater Pike
(Centropomus undecimalis)

This is a pugnacious-looking, hard-fighting, popular fish that on light tackle is a real challenge. Not easy to catch, snook are worth the effort as they make a great meal. Preferred water temperature: 70°-86° F. All-tackle record: 53 lb 10 oz.

WHERE AND WHEN

1. Atlantic coast, especially the Fort Pierce, Jupiter, and Sebastian Inlets but along the beaches, as well. Snook bite best spring through fall, especially during a full moon and at night and very early morning. Salt marshes offering good fishing for snook can be found from St. Augustine to Marineland. But here, as in Ponce Inlet, Mosquito Lagoon, and other more northerly places, expect action in the fall and early winter only if the weather is mild. No matter what the weather is, some of the best snook fishing is at night under the Intracoastal Waterway bridges from Stuart to Boca Raton.
2. Upper Keys, Everglades, and Ten Thousand Islands, May through August. As it cools in November, the fish move from the passes and more open water to back country

holes, deep canals, creek mouths, and in depressions under mangrove branches.

3. Gulf coast to about the Tampa Bay area, although some fish are caught a little farther north. October is good in the Tampa Bay region but, in general, May through September during the full and new moon phases is the time to fish, especially in the surf from Longboat Key to Naples and in passes such as Captiva, Redfish, and Stump—try during the middle of a flood or ebb tide. When it cools off in October or November, the estuarine rivers such as the Peace and Myakka are good choices: snook sometimes go as far up as freshwater when it is very cold. A productive place at such a time is a power plant outfall. An unusually cold winter and spring keeps snook in this back country, miles from open saltwater. Because of the sun's position at this time of the year, look for fish in the warmer water of the north and northwest shores of bays, lagoons, and river mouths. In all of their range, residential canals during cold weather are locations where snook seek warm water.

TACKLE

Spinning and Plug Casting. Rods about 7'; line 8#-30#, mono or braided; spin or conventional reel.

Surf and Inlet. Because of rough surf and inlets' rapid currents and jetty rocks, heavy equipment is necessary. 8'-9' medium-to-heavy rod; 20#-30# line, mono or braided; spin or conventional reel holding at least 200 yd of line.

Fly. 8½' rod, 8 or 9 weight; weight-forward, floating line and a fast sinking one, as well; 100 yd of 20# Dacron backing.

TECHNIQUES

Atlantic Coast Inlets

Natural Bait

Shrimp: At Sebastian and Fort Pierce Inlets, fishing a live shrimp during the ebb tide, especially the first part of it, and from

March through May, is the way to catch the largest snook of the year. Whether in a boat or on foot, one must move around until the fish are found, and this not only includes the inside inlet area but also outside of the channel where the jetty and beach come together. Although the best time is during dark, early in the day is good, too, and has the advantage that in clear water fish can be spotted. Or a depth finder can be used any time. If fishing from a boat and away from rocks, try lighter tackle such as a 10#-20# outfit with a 2′ 40# leader; go heavier—up to a 60# leader—if fishing from shore and over rocks. Using a 1/0-2/0 Mustad O'Shaughnessy hook, impale a shrimp under the horn on top of its head. The objective is to fish the shrimp near the bottom so during slack or slow tides, only a couple of split shot weights above the swivel attaching leader to line are necessary. But when the tide is strong, attach a ½ oz-5/8 oz egg sinker in the same place.

Bait fish: When shrimp become scarce in late April, use live bait fish. Mullet, the nearly universal bait, are always productive and, as with other live bait, should be used during an ebb tide. When other bait fishes are present, snook often confine their feeding to the species making an appearance. This includes the following fishes at one time or place or another: menhaden, spots, goggle eyes, pilchards, and pinfish. Depending upon the species, these bait fishes can be caught with a cast net, seine, or on hook and line (see the live bait section—p. 154—on how to catch each bait fish desired). It is often necessary to catch bait in an entirely different place from where the snook are running, but near each inlet there is usually a good place and you can get its location from a local bait and tackle store. The main criteria regarding which bait to go after are whether it is abundant at the time and can easily live in the bait well. Much bait is sometimes necessary as reluctant snook can often be thrown into a feeding frenzy by chumming live bait, a dozen or so every few minutes. Because snook will drop natural bait if they feel any resistance, drifting in a boat while freelining the bait is the best technique; you may need a few split shot weights to keep the bait deep. Where there is anything on the bottom such as rocks or debris that would tangle a free-running live bait, the short sliding sinker rig is used. Use about a 3/0-6/0 short-shank hook and attach it to the swivel with

1½'-2' of 40#-60# mono. Hook the bait fish ahead of or behind the dorsal fin, through the lips, or only through the upper lip if it's a mullet.

Artificial Bait

Spin and plug: Double the fishing line with a Bimini Twist loop as long as the fishing rod. Leaders should be short enough to facilitate comfortable casting and heavy enough—up to 50# or 60#—when fishing near rocks. Artificials are most productive at night during an ebb tide, but it is wise to find out locally when is the prime time. Artificials should be cast in the direction of the current and slowly retrieved, imparting little action, just swimming them back as the current swings them down. Large plugs with a big lip can be rapidly reeled in for a few feet to get them deep and then retrieved slowly. The locally made Red-Tailed Hawk is a bucktail jig in white with some red and is used with great success but any white feather jig with a plastic worm of any color attached will work. Plugs in chartreuse, red and white, and white or silver with black backs are effective. Use the 7" Rebel Redfin; a Rapala Magnum; the Model A Magnum Bomber; the Trader Bay Snook Slayer; and Mirrolures 85M, 82M, 98MR, and 72M. With lots of bait in an inlet during a slack tide, use a floating plug.

Trolling: Slowly trolling large plugs such as the ones listed above or a de-boned mullet are good inlet techniques during an ebb tide and are designed to avoid the crowds often found lining the banks of inlets when the word gets out that snook are running.

Spillways

Along the Atlantic coast parallel to the Everglades and Lake Okeechobee locks control water drainage to the ocean. After much rain, usually near the end of summer, thousands of gallons of water are dumped daily into canals that empty into the Intracoastal Waterway, which eventually, through the inlets, carries the Glades' water to sea. As the water cascades through the locks, bait fish are carried along and in the resulting brackish water snook have a picnic eating their way through the sudden food bonanza. Anglers have a picnic, too. Fish, of course, when water is dumped, but your chances are best if it is early morning.

Natural Bait. Live shrimp are alright, but by far the best live bait is the gizzard shad, a small fish one must cast-net in freshwater. However, they do not easily survive transportation and must be kept uncrowded in lots of aerated water. An alternative bait is the freshwater shiner that can be bought in bait and tackle stores, but they don't live very long in the brackish water of a spillway. Use a 2/0-5/0 hook and impale a shrimp under the horn on the head and a bait fish through the upper back around the dorsal fin or through the nose or lips. 20# line with a 2' 30#-50# leader is about right. Sometimes a float is used. Cast into the current and let the bait drift. A mullet head fished on the bottom works, too.

Artificial Bait. Although not as effective as natural bait in a spillway, artificials do catch fish. Use a tout or a feather jig in white with a red plastic worm tail; after casting, let it sink to the bottom and retrieve slowly.

Bridges, Piers, and Docks

These are natural places for snook to hide to grab a meal. Where the water is deep, fish during the last few hours of the ebb and the first part of the flood tides. The slack, low water between these tides is often a time when snook feed. Where the water is shallow, the reverse is better: the last of the flood and first of the ebb as well as the slack high. If fishing from a bridge, pick a tide when the automobile traffic diminishes, about 10 p.m. or later. Don't worry if there's a light shining on the water; it not only attracts bait, but it helps the angler see the action.

Natural Bait. Tackle should be heavy enough to pull snook away from barnacle-encrusted pilings. 50# line is about right (although it may be light for a large fish) with a 2'-3' mono leader to 80#. Heavy leaders inhibit a live bait's action so lighter mono may be necessary. If the fish are small, lighter tackle can be used. Using a short-shank 1/0-3/0, hook a large shrimp through the horn or a live fish in front of the dorsal fin or through the lips (only the upper lip, if mullet). Baits that stay deep such as pilchards, pinfish, and sand perch are the best. Fish on the upcurrent side and free spool the line so that the water carries the bait along the edge or under the bridge or pier. If a bait is allowed to drag in a current on a taut line, it will look unnatural and will be rejected by a snook.

Artificial Bait. Cast upcurrent and retrieve slowly with the flow of water. If fishing from a boat at a bridge whose spans are wide, go downcurrent of it and cast upcurrent under the bridge. Any artificial bait listed above under inlet fishing is okay. At Gulf coast bridges local fishermen favor the following artificials: Bomber plugs, 16 and 17 series; the Magnum Rapala; and jigs.

Surf

Natural Bait. During the night in April and then all through the summer early in the morning to 10 a.m. on a flood tide are prime times when snook can be caught in the surf. The best location is a beach no more than a few hundred yards from an inlet or pass and around the sandbars and groins. Cast up to 50′ out and try to keep the bait in the undertow region of receding waves. Live finger mullet and white bait are the best baits although other bait fishes will work. Using a fish finder rig and with a 6/0, hook a live bait behind the anal fin or, if there is a heavy surf, through the upper lip. A school of tarpon in the surf often has snook beneath them; hook a live bait under the throat latch to drive it deep to where the fish lie or weigh it down with an ounce or two of lead.

Artificial Bait. The time to fish is the same as when using natural bait, but less light is even more important when fishing with artificials. Cast as parallel to the beach as possible and swim the lure back slowly. All the lures listed under inlet fishing are possibilities, but along the central and lower Atlantic coast, Krocodile or Gator spoons are used. Plugs colored dark green or chartreuse work well, too. Along the Gulf coast barrier beaches at Sanibel and Captiva Islands, blue-backed Rat-L-Traps are a good choice. Jigs bounced off the sandy bottom catch fish, also.

Mangrove Islands, Gulf Coast Passes, and Back Country

Natural Bait. Fishing the Gulf coast passes is much like Atlantic coast inlets. Ebb tide, especially the last three hours, nighttime, and shrimp or pilchards are the best combinations and the bait should be freelined and used with a 3′ 30# mono leader. See Atlantic coast inlets, p. 117, for other rigging information. Pilchards can be cast netted over grass flats; the deeper the water, the larger the net must be. Pinfish are one of the best baits here. In the passes the spot to fish is the dropoff near the channel edge and although this can be done from the shore, the really successful fishermen use boats and drift. Electric motors are a good idea to get back to start another drift without making a lot of noise. Mangroves, wherever found, should be explored as snook frequently hide beneath the branches, mainly in the deeper holes. As with trout and redfish, snook prefer bottom structure; any kind of rubble is fine but oyster bars are generally fished, especially where they meet an island or where a creek flows into them and there is an ebb tide. Back country fishing is primarily in creeks, rivers, and bays whose water ranges from brackish to fresh. Ledges along the shoreline and deep holes in the bottom where the water is not dirty are places to look; cast into such places and be careful not to bring the boat too close.

Spin and Plug Casting. Fish the same places and times as above. Because of mangroves and bottom structure, leaders of a comfortable casting length made from at least 30# mono are required; if the water is dirty and mangrove roots are a problem, you can go to 50#. There are quite a variety of successful lures to choose from. In clear water try plugs with blue or black tops and silver sides; in dirty water, go for bright colors such as yellow and red combinations. A red head and white body plug is one of the oldest yet most productive. Use heavier lures where the current is swift. Work bucktails and touts right on the bottom, bouncing them up and down during the retrieve. Among the best are Rat-L-Traps; the Castana and Spinana; Bagley's Finger Mullet; the Zara Spook; the Purple Demon, 7M, and Copperhead Mirrolures; red head and white bodied jigs; yellow bucktails, touts such as the Cotee Gold-Glitter Shad or one with a root beer tail when the water is dirty; the silver Rapala and Rebel; and skimmer jigs with a 2″ mullet strip attached. In canals when it is cold, use a slowly retrieved Mirrolure TT or 52M with a green back and light belly. Also try a gold spoon with a bit of red nailpolish at its front end.

Fly. Use a 6' or 7' leader with a 16# tippet plus 1' of 30# mono as a shock leader. When in a boat and casting up against a mangrove-lined shore, plan casts so that the line is at a right angle with the shore; this will allow a little more pulling power than is possible with a cast somewhat parallel to shore. Good-size fly rod lures have a 1/0-3/0 hook. Popping bugs are excellent, particularly when fish are under mangroves, and should be worked by retrieving at a moderate speed, popping the bug every few feet. Sliders are effective in clear, shallow water and should be used with a 12' leader; retrieve with long strips.

The Dahlberg Diver, worked fast enough to create a wake, is an effective fly. And Deceiver and Seaducer types in white with some blue or green, white and red, yellow and red, and yellow and grizzly are fine. Under mangroves allow these streamers to sink before beginning the retrieve. Any other time, strip them about a foot at a time and keep them moving; speed up when a fish approaches. Also try the Bend Back River Shrimp, 3"-4" long. Although it's not saltwater fishing, the Everglades and Tamiami Trail freshwater canals, far from the ocean but nevertheless connected to it, are good places for small fly rod snook. Two to three inch streamers in patterns as above will work very well; lighter tackle is in order for these fish. An especially productive place for nighttime snook fly fishing is under dock lights; use a green and white streamer and fish it in the shadows as well as you can. When fishing a canal or pass and you suspect the fish are lying on the bottom, use a fast-sinking line and a bend back fly, keeping it deep with a slow retrieve.

How to Hook a Snook. With artificials it is necessary to set the hook at the instant the strike is felt. With live bait, however, allow the fish to run four or five seconds. Simply throw the reel in free spool and allow the fish to move away with the bait in its mouth. After striking, exert enough pressure to keep the fish's head pointing at you as line allowed to cross the head of a snook will probably cut on the sharp gill covers. If the fish tries to swim for entangling cover, keep the pressure on so the battle can be fought in open water.

How to Land a Snook. Some of the best snook fishing is during the closed season (perfectly within the law), and catches must be released. If a fish is to be kept, use a net. If the fish is hooked in the mouth and can be easily reached, use pliers on the hook shank and back it out. If the hook has been swallowed, using gloves heavy enough so the teeth will not pierce, thumb the lower jaw to hold the mouth open. Cut the line as close to the hook as possible; bronze hooks, if used, will rust in a short time, leaving the fish unharmed. Be very careful while handling a live snook; the gill covers, as mentioned already, are razor sharp. If the fish seems exhausted, hold it so that the water flow enters the mouth and move it back and forth; when it revives, release it.

Other Fish Caught While Fishing for Snook. Jack crevalle, redfish, spotted seatrout, ladyfish, and tarpon.

Regulations

- Closed Season: December 15 through January 31; June 1 through August 31
- Minimum Size: 24″ overall
- Maximum Size: 34″ overall (only one fish this size or longer allowed
- Daily Bag Limit: 2
- Note: In addition to a saltwater fishing license, a special snook stamp must be purchased. Snook must be brought in with head and fins intact.

27

Striped Bass; Striper; Rockfish
(Morone saxatilis)

A fish that is better known in the northeast part of the United States, the striped bass spends most of its time in salt and brackish water but swims far up into rivers to spawn. It is considered a delicious fish for eating. Preferred water temperature: 56°-77° F. All-tackle record: 78 lb 8 oz (in Florida fish over 38 lb have been caught).

WHERE AND WHEN

1. From the Georgia border to the St. Johns River from November to the peak month, March, stripers are caught around bridges in Jacksonville in at least 8′ of water. In addition, during the summer spawning run into freshwater, they can be caught up the St. Johns at Welaka and at Lake Monroe which is north of Orlando. The best time to fish the mouth of the St. Johns is early and late in the day (at night, too) and when it is overcast; the weather should be cool to cold. The first part of both the flood and ebb tides are right and you should be on the downtide side of a bridge.

2. From the Alabama border to the Suwannee River in the northwest part of the state, striper fishing is possible but not nearly as good as in the St. Johns River. However, in December 1990, 25,000 striped bass were stocked in the Apalachicola River and a school of stripers was observed from the pier at Fort Walton Beach in March so Panhandle fishing might improve.

TACKLE

Spinning and Plug Casting. A 6½'-9' rod; 20#-25# line, mono or braided; spin or conventional reel.

TECHNIQUES

Natural Bait. The best bait for striped bass has always been eels, but they do eat bait fish such as shiners. Although most of Florida striper fishing is done with artificials, if you can find a source for live eels, hook one about 8" long through the eye socket with a 3/0-4/0 hook and either freeline it or attach about a ½ oz-1 oz egg sinker, depending on the current, above the swivel. Use strong equipment such as a 3' leader of 30#-40# mono, because the fishing is deep around bridge pilings that have sharp barnacles growing upon them. Docks and pilings fished where the current is swift is another place you can catch stripers. Move around to find fish; don't anchor and expect them to find you.

Artificial Bait. Fish in the same locations as above but use the following lures with a leader as above: a Rapala Shad Rap; a 6" red and white Bomber Long A; a ½ oz Cotee jig with an 8" grubtail; an eelskin (obtainable only in the North); an 8" black plastic worm rigged Texas-style with lead ahead of it; and, for the surface, the Bagley Bangolure.

Other Fish Caught While Fishing for Striped Bass. Bluefish, spotted seatrout, and flounder.

Regulations

Striped bass are considered freshwater fish in Florida and therefore to fish for them a freshwater license is required. There is a limit of 20 fish, and not more than 6 can be over 24" overall.

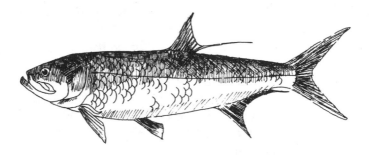

28

Tarpon; Silver King; Silver Sides; Sabalo

(Megalops atlanticus)

Certainly the most spectacular, acrobatic fish of them all, the tarpon can jump ten feet out of the water, twisting its limber body while rattling its great gills. Although it is edible, it is not very tasty; the attraction of this magnificent battler is the great fight that makes it so difficult to land. Preferred water temperature: 74°–88°F. All-tackle record: 283 lb 4 oz.

WHERE AND WHEN

1. Upper and Middle Keys, especially bridges such as at Channel Two and Five, Tom's Harbor, Long Key, the east end of the Seven Mile Bridge, and flats areas such as Jack Bank near Marathon and Buchanan Bank near Islamorada Key. Mid-March through mid-July is the peak time. Anglers begin to find tarpon on the flats of the Florida Bay side of the Keys during mid-March and by June far more fish are on the Atlantic side. Fish are present year-round but not in such great quantity.

2. Lower Keys, in particular Key West Harbor, the Marquesas Keys, and the Bahia Honda Bridge. For most of the Lower Keys, May, June, and July are the best months but fish will be found all year. The unique tarpon fishing in Key West Harbor sometimes starts in January and is very good in February and March. The Marquesas lie beyond Key West and are not connected by road. Their inaccessibility offers virgin tarpon fishing April through July. Several days before the first full moon in June, there is a hatch of the palolo worm, a reef dweller at the Bahia Honda Bridge. The eggs float to the surface and stimulate all fish, including tarpon, into a feeding frenzy.

3. Everglades National Park and the Ten Thousand Island region, especially locations such as Sandy Key and Rabbit Key Basins; the canals at both ends of Lake Ingraham; the mouths of Harney and Lostmans rivers; and the Turner River at Chokoloskee. This famous fishing location offers tarpon all year with the largest fish being caught from March to July during the last half of an ebb tide, both early and late in the day.

4. West coast from the Everglades National Park north all the way to the Panhandle. In this stretch of coast is the most famous, long-time center for tarpon—Boca Grande—where the time to try is May and June when literally thousands of fish are caught. A little farther north, offshore of the Crystal River in Homosassa Bay, there is superb flats fishing for very large tarpon which starts the first of May and lasts to mid-June. Such northerly spots as Apalachicola Bay are good all summer beginning at the end of June.

5. Atlantic coast from Biscayne Bay north, especially large inlets such as Miami's Government Cut and Port Everglades from around January through June and coastal beaches during August and September. Although tarpon are caught along the entire Atlantic coast of Florida, the southern half of the state offers the best fishing.

TACKLE

Spinning and Plug Casting. In open water where there are no obstructions, light tackle is not only possible but is sensational fun. Use about a 7′ rod; 12#-15# line, mono or braided; spin or conventional reel to hold at least 250 yd. Where mangrove roots, piers, and bridges can foul the fishing line, go heavier with a 7′-8′ rod; 30# line or heavier, mono or braided; spin or conventional reel to hold at least 150 yd.

Inlet and Surf. 8′-9′ rod; 30#-50# line, mono or braided; a reel to hold at least 300 yd, either a 4/0 conventional type or a heavy-duty spinning reel.

Fly. A 9′-9½′ rod, 11-13 weight; weight-forward or shooting head floating line and an intermediate sinking line; a high-grade reel with a quality drag system and which can hold 300 yd of 30# Dacron backing plus a 100′ length of 25# mono shock absorber tied between the fishing line and the backing.

TECHNIQUES

Keys

Bridge Fishing

Natural bait: Nighttime fishing during the ebb tide is the right time but some fish are caught during the day. Boat fishermen should position themselves upcurrent and drift the bait to the bridge. With a Bimini Twist, double the end of the fishing line about 6′ and attach 6′-10′ of 100# mono, either with a swivel or directly to the line, with an Albright Special knot. Hooks must be very sharp to penetrate a tarpon's bony mouth.

- Shrimp: Using an Eagle Claw #254N, about 2/0-4/0, hook a large shrimp under the horn on the head or thread it on the hook. Freeline it; a float inhibits the shrimp's swimming. Chumming with cut-up pieces of shrimp helps.
- Fish: Pilchards, mullet, and pinfish are the best baits to use. With an Eagle Claw #85, a Mustad 7690 or 7691 anywhere from 6/0-10/0 depending on bait size, if at anchor hook a mullet inside the upper lip and out the top of the head; some fishermen split the lower lip to facilitate breathing. If drifting, hook any of the bait fishes in front of the dorsal fin or behind the anal fin. Use a large float 6′-8′ above the bait.

Attach the float by doubling the line through it and holding it in place with a golf tee or similar device. Any hook used should have an offset point for easier penetration and you can use pliers to bend one slightly. Another hook to try with live bait is the Mustad circle hook, size 3, 4, or 5. As odd as this hook may appear, its percentage of hook-ups is higher than with conventional hooks; this is important with tarpon as only one out of five fish hooked is brought to gaff.

Artificial bait: Follow the same directions as above regarding tide and location.

- Spin and Plug: Shorten the leader to a length comfortable for casting and the following lures, worked very slowly, can be used: a 3-oz Gator spoon; jigs with a small piece of shrimp on the hook; the Mirrolure 66M18 or the 85M 18 or 21; and the Creek Chub Wiggle Diver. Slow trolling alongside bridges with a Magnum Rapala or other large plug is effective. At Bahia Honda Bridge during the palolo worm hatch in June, hungry fish can be caught in all the ways suggested.
- Fly: Fishing close to a bridge with flies is self-defeating as the fisherman has no pulling power to avoid losing a fish on a piling. If fish are feeding over more open water as at Bahia Honda during the worm hatch, then fly-rodding can be great: an all-orange fly suggests the reef worm eggs. Otherwise, use flies listed under flats fishing for tarpon.

Flats Fishing

Flats 5'-10' deep are fished from boats specially designed for the job, but any small skiff or rowboat will work. Because tarpon flush at noises, get the boat close to spotted small pods or large schools of fish by push-poling or by using an electric motor.

Natural bait

- Shrimp: use the largest obtainable and fish with the same rig as at a bridge. Cast to a sighted fish somewhat ahead of it and raise the rod tip as soon as the shrimp touches water, causing it to skip across the surface attracting tarpon. Keep casting until you get a fish's attention.

- Crabs: Remove claws with pliers and also break off the two sharp points at the sides of the top shell. Pass a shrimp hook through the shell near the broken-off point from bottom up and out through the top. Cast ahead of a tarpon and, just as with the shrimp, bring the crab back on the water's surface, stopping and letting it sink to the bottom right in front of the fish.
- Fish: Live or dead fish and particularly a large mullet head fished on the bottom are good baits. Use the same rig as with bridge fishing, with the float adjusted so that the live bait is above the grass but unable to get into it and hide. Because of the weight involved, casting such a rig with light tackle is nearly impossible so heavier bridge or surf equipment is preferable. Once again, cast in front of the sighted tarpon; the splashing around of the somewhat stunned live bait is what attracts. If a pod of tarpon is swimming in a circle (called a "daisy chain"), don't startle them with a poor cast; drop the bait to the outside of the circle where fish will see it while circling.

Artificial bait: Flats fishing is the great location for using artificials and fish nearly 200 lb have been caught on a fly rod. The use of light line in casting makes flats fishing very effective as tarpon are not so easily flushed with long, delicate casts. As with the fishing discussed above, artificials should be tossed in front of a sighted fish close enough for the lure to be seen. In very calm water this critical distance should be somewhat greater so as not to frighten the fish.

- Spin and Plug: Double the line for a few feet with a Bimini Twist, and with an Albright Special knot, attach 2' or 3' of 40# mono, and, between the end of this and the lure and with the same knot, tie on a 12" piece of 80#-100# mono as a shock leader. It would be better if the 40# mono part could be lengthened but it would interfere with casting. However, a longer rod will facilitate the use of a longer leader. For lures, there are many to choose from as this great sport fish has attracted inventive minds for years. Bill Smith tarpon lures in orange and white and orange and yellow should be, as with all tarpon lures, retrieved slowly by moving the rod tip a little to the side, reeling in line, and repeating. The

Mirrolure 88M in red and yellow should be quietly chugged through the water, floating and sinking just beneath the surface. The Mirrolure 66M18 should be allowed to sink after casting and then slowly retrieved by long pulls of the rod tip, the angler pausing to reel in slack line, and repeating. The 52M Mirrolure and the Bagley Sinking Finger Mullet in natural brown or silver are worth trying. Also try 6" Texas-rigged worms in black, green, or red and worked slowly near the bottom.

- Fly: The same searching and sighting procedures as already discussed should be followed. Leaders must vary with the situation: consider 9' as normal and either buy one commercially made or put one together as follows: 6' 40#, 2' class tippet 12# or 16#, and 1' 80# shock. When it is calm and the water is clear or early in the morning over sand, up to 14' of leader may be necessary; in this case, lengthen the butt section. If the water is choppy, a 4' leader will sometimes work. The deeper you fish, the shorter it must be, as long leaders and sinking lines are incompatible; 3' might be enough. "Baby" tarpon—fish under 50 lb—and even larger ones occasionally can be handled on 5' of 50# mono leader alone.

On the flats the color of fly to use depends somewhat on the bottom make-up, but they should be 3"-5" long, #2-2/0 hooks for baby tarpon, and up to 5/0 for large fish. The Cockroach, a brown bucktail with grizzly feathers, offers good contrast with a sandy bottom, and other streamer-types in orange, orange and yellow, and red and yellow do the same. Over a dark grass bottom streamers colored light gray or blue and green are effective. When tarpon are feeding on mullet, 7"-9" white flies with dark backs work. Popping bugs in red and white are good. Some people successfully use crab imitations. Probably more important than the fly type is how it is retrieved. Work it in 6"-12" slow strips, pausing and jerking; if a fish follows, shorten the strips and speed them up to produce a frightened fish action.

Key West Harbor. A large population of tarpon live here during the winter but only while it is warm. A cold front will drive them out to the reef but they can be expected to return, rolling their way back to the Harbor, a few days after the cold weather has passed. Fish in the morning or afternoon, when the tide is slowly ebbing, in about 40′ of water in the main ship channel and south of Tank Island; also fish on a flood tide in the channel going to Garrison Bight. There will be no problem locating the hot spots since many boats will be in the middle of them already. Even if tarpon are rolling at the surface, the action is deep and pods of fish can be located with a depth finder. Anchor upcurrent of fish and chum with shrimp heads or trash obtained from shrimpers that have just completed a drag; you may have to go many miles out in the Gulf to find such a fishing boat. Or you can chum with frozen ground-up menhaden mixed with cut pieces of fresh fish. 20#-30# line is about right and a 50# mono leader up to 6′ is necessary.

Natural bait: Bury a hook up to 5/0 in one of the crabs or mantis shrimps from the trash, in a large shrimp you have bought, or in a pinfish you have caught. Let it float down with the chum. Or, using a 4/0 hook through both lips of a mojarra (shad or sand bream locally) with some lead above the swivel connecting line to leader, fish on the bottom. Strikes are surprisingly gentle and not easily felt so at any movement of the line, set the hook hard.

Artificial bait: Use a short, yellow or white round-headed, nylon, pompano-style jig up to 2 oz with or without a plastic tail. It can be fished by drifting and casting, allowing the jig to sink and retrieving it with either long up-and-down sweeps of the rod tip or short pulls, always keeping it near the bottom where the fish are holding.

Inlets and Passes

Outside. On both coasts tarpon school off of beaches in water from a few feet deep to 40′ or 50′. They are therefore accessible to both surf fishermen and boat anglers.

Gulf coast: Beaches of Captiva, Sanibel, and Estero islands and on down to Naples are places outside of which fishermen cruise in boats spotting schools of tarpon in 20′-40′ of water. The fish are usually rolling on the surface or swimming in a circular "daisy chain" and the boat must approach quietly (a good time for an electric motor) and anchor either ahead of where the school seems to be moving or upcurrent of the fish. Use chum, either live menhaden or chunks from this fish or any other oily kind such as mullet. Pinfish are the most commonly used bait and they are rigged as with bridge fishing but with 4/0-7/0 hooks; that is, place a large float 6'-8' above the bait and use 100# mono in-between. Other bait such as scaled sardines (shiners), mutton minnows (mojarra), sand perch (squirrel fish), large shrimp, and crabs are also used. A long rod is necessary to cast such a load and this is usually done by a 360° roundhouse swing from the top of the boat's tower. A 4/0 reel with 36# nylon squidding line is a local favorite combination. Cast ahead of moving fish. When the float disappears, point the rod tip at where it was, reel in line until you feel weight and set the hook hard—only a very sharp hook can penetrate the bony mouth of a tarpon. Artificials such as a jig with a chartreuse skirt, the Mirrolure 66M18, and red and white plugs do work, but live bait is definitely superior.

Atlantic coast: On beaches along central and south Florida after a northeaster in August, September, and early October, the wind swings to the east and mullet and other bait fishes come close to shore, sometimes in such shallow water they can easily be captured with a cast net. If they are too far out for this, cast a snatch hook, a weighted treble hook, into the school with a stout surf rod and sweep the rod tip back in large arcs to snag a mullet. Bait caught this way may be left out to sink to the bottom to attract a tarpon. However, they may not be securely hooked so it is best to bring them in quickly and keep them in a bucket of water until used. Hook mullet through the upper lip, add a 1 oz-4 oz weight, and, using no float, cast out to tarpon swimming about. Whole dead bait can be fished on the surface by pumping air into them with a large hypodermic needle hooked up to a bicycle pump. Or you can fish mullet or bluefish heads on the bottom. This kind of fishing requires a 50# leader plus 1' of 80#-100# mono shock, the total length of which should not exceed what is comfortable for casting. If near an inlet, fish the ebb tide, but when there is a lot of bait in the water, try the first part of the flood tide, as well. Artificials can be used: a 5/8 oz white jig with a 4" red or green plastic worm; a Hopkins or a Krocodile spoon; a Magnum Rapala; and the Mirrolure 60M, 66M, and 85M, all with green or black backs and white bellies.

Inside. Along both coasts the tide runs from the ocean to inshore water and back again, each time carrying with it all manner of swimming food.

Atlantic coast inlets: At night and early in the morning on the ebb tide just before a full or new moon and during the first five months of the year as long as the water is at least 74° F., a special kind of deep-water fishing for tarpon in the 100-lb class occurs in the large inlets along the South Florida shore. Use a depth finder as the boat zig-zags from inside the inlet—usually near the jetties—to one-half mile beyond the inlet's mouth. When fish are found, position the boat upcurrent of where they are holding and drift down over the fish.

- Natural bait: Large live shrimp attached to a jig head, mullet, and pinfish also weighted to sink are used and, as already explained, a long, heavy mono leader is necessary. Allow these baits to sink, bring them up slowly and repeat.
- Artificial bait: Try the following: the Mirrolure 85M and 65M in pink; green or orange-tail jigs to 1 oz worked slowly up and down from bottom to surface; and other deep lures as recommended for bridge fishing. The fly rodder can work here, too, but must use a rapid-sink line or a shooting head of at least 750 grains, white or red streamer flies (black if the water is dirty) on 4/0 hooks. It can not be repeated too often that artificials must be retrieved slowly to catch tarpon.

Gulf coast passes: Because of numerous small barrier islands lining the coast up to Tampa Bay, there are many sensational places to look for tarpon. Some locations can be waded on a low tide while others are the deepest places where tarpon are fished.

- Boca Grande: This is one of the oldest but hottest spots to catch tarpon in Florida. Although fish are in this region all year, they very reliably appear in May and June in not only great numbers but great size, as well. They are caught during both ebb and flood tides, especially early and late in the day. Although light tackle can be used, fishing is deep so a 5½'-6' stand-up rod with a 4/0 or 6/0 conventional reel loaded with 50# mono or braided line (or, better yet, non-stretching Dacron) is correct gear. Short-shank hooks, 4/0-6/0, a 7' or 8' piece of 100# mono or #7 piano wire leader, and a break-away sinker are necessary. The sinker can be the egg-type from ½ oz-8 oz, depending on the depth fished.

Pass a piece of copper rigging wire through it and attach one end to the swivel that connects line to leader, and wrap the other end a few times around the leader. Then mark the line by wrapping it a few turns with unwaxed dental tape that you have colored with an indelible felt-tip pen or with a few drops of nail polish. Mark the depth or depths you will fish: 45'-50' is right for Boca Grande Pass while for the Tarpon Hole, a trench outside the Pass, 70' is correct. Still another region of the Pass called the Hump is in 20' of water and, being so shallow, produces far more acrobatic fish. Three inch wide ("dollar" size they call them locally) blue crabs are the best nighttime bait and can be hand-netted as they float in Charlotte Harbor on the surface during an ebb tide near sunset. Once the claws are removed, the crabs should be hooked under a point at the side of the shell and out the top. Large shrimp, sand perch, or other local fishes are good, too, and should be taken on the fishing trip because tarpon are notoriously picky. Hook the shrimp through the horn and the fish through the lips.

The first step in making a drift over located fish, with the baits suspended at the marked depth, is to carefully observe how the other boats are handling the traffic problem. With one person at the controls at all times, cruise to the upcurrent end of the fishing fleet, shift the engine into neutral, and drift with the tide. At the end of the drift, repeat, but always keep the engine at idle to quickly get away from a collision situation, to speed up to set the hook, and to snake out of the fleet with a hooked tarpon on the line. Artificials work sometimes. Try a 1-oz orange tout; a Cotee Liv'Eye jig with a green tail; a Tarpon Taker jig up to 3 oz (there is a glow model for nighttime fishing); and Mirrolures such as the

65M and 67M with as much red, gold, and orange or fluorescent colors on them as possible. Work these slowly as close to the bottom as you can.

- Other passes: Such passes as Redfish, Captiva, and others offer both deep- and shallow-water tarpon fishing. The top of an ebb tide is a good time to try, and any of the techniques already described will catch fish if you recognize that rather than hunting fish you will be looking for such bottom irregularities as holes, drop-offs, or other such places that offer waiting fish protection while looking for food. Bait fish caught in a current of outgoing water at the mouth of the pass frequently makes this the most productive spot.

Bays, Rivers, and Canals

In the southern part of the state in a body of water such as Charlotte Harbor, anglers find some of the best year-round tarpon fishing. Even though the peak is from May through August and sometimes even later, at any time of the year fish can be found some place in this large body of water. There are bridge pilings, grass flats, and mangrove islands which, especially at night during spring tides, offer excellent fishing. Frequently tarpon are deep beneath branches of mangroves lining the land in the bay. Casting bait close in, especially noisy varieties, catches fish.

Both shrimp and bait fishes can be used as they make enough commotion to attract fish and artificials that do the same such as chugger plugs and a popping bug for the fly rodder is a good choice. Gently shaking the mangrove branches with a long pole will often send hiding tarpon out and present the caster with a specific target. Later on, in the fall and winter, rivers feeding bays are home to huge schools of tarpon. Baits already mentioned will work but also try bottom fishing with catfish you have captured on pieces of mullet or ladyfish caught on jigs. Large plugs trolled far behind the boat are also effective. Biscayne Bay's Turkey Point cooling canals are winter gathering places for tarpon. Apalachicola Bay tarpon in the summer are attracted by cut bait or a mullet head fished on the bottom. Canal fishing for baby tarpon is well worth trying. Any canal connected to salt water up to central Florida is a possibility, but those along the Tamiami Trail, Marco Road, the Loxahatchee area, and State Road 84 (Alligator Alley) are well known for lots of small fish. March to November on an ebb tide is the time to fish; spin and plug casters can go down to 12# line or less, 1′ of 40# and 1′ of 80# mono for a leader and shock, and 1/0 or 2/0 hooks if using live bait. Artificials can be the small Rapala, the small Rebel, and round-headed crappie jigs about 1/8 oz. Fly rodders can use a 5-7 weight rod, a 10# tippet with a 20# 12″ shock, a #1 or 1/0 1″-2″ streamer in white or yellow, the Dahlberg Diver, a Marabou streamer, muddler flies, and all-black streamers in this dirty water; place the fly right on the nose of a rising fish.

Gulf Coast Offshore Flats

The world's best tarpon fly fishermen convene off Crystal River and Homosassa to fish the offshore flats every year in May and June. For you to do so, see the flats fishing information above as described for the Keys, p. 130.

How to Hook a Tarpon. Anglers frequently measure how good a fishing day it has been by stating how many tarpon they "jumped," not landed, a reference to the very bony mouth which is difficult to penetrate with a hook. The solution to this is not to rely on hooks straight out of the box being sharp enough; use a good grade file to sharpen the points. Another problem in hooking a tarpon is the strike: it is usually too soon. With natural bait, take in slack line and strike hard twice on the hit. Because tarpon suck in food including much water at the same time, some fishermen wait a second or two until the fish rolls over before striking as that indicates the bait is solidly in its mouth. With a hard lure, strike as soon as you feel a heavy weight at the end of the line.

In fly fishing for tarpon, most fishermen strike when they see the fish eat the fly and that is too soon—don't set the hook until you feel a weight at the end of the line just as described. If a tarpon takes a fly while following it, stop stripping for an instant to let the fly go deep into the fish's mouth; then set the hook. If the fish takes the fly while swimming towards you, strike several times in quick succession. Always set the hook by keeping the rod tip close to the water and, with the rod butt tight in your belly, rotate your body, making the rod move sideways while the line hand strips in hard. If drift fishing as at Boca Grande and elsewhere, set the hook by suddenly and rapidly going ahead with the boat. In spite of all your efforts at hook-setting, the exploding fish will shake free most of the time.

How to Land a Tarpon. Once a fish is solidly hooked, and in the eruption that follows does not free itself, expect high jumps, somersaults, and gill-rattling fury at being held. One hopes this action will occur some distance from the boat because a hundred pounds or more of thrashing fish dropping into the boat with the angler can be a disaster. In any event, the fisherman must "bow" to a leaping tarpon, and this means lowering the rod tip to the horizontal and pushing it ahead to quickly give slack. There is no holding such a large, active fish and no "horsing" it in, either. Control is the key word and reel brake systems need help, such as holding your fingers so that the line is pressed to the rod as it is pulled out by the fish. When a tarpon is exhausted and can be brought in, it usually signifies this by rolling on its side. Using a short lip gaff, pass it through the lower lip and the fish will be held while someone removes the hook or clips the leader as close to it as possible. However, large fish lifted by a lip gaff can be injured so they should be allowed to remain in the water and the hook removed from that position. Because nearly all tarpon are released, some fishermen flatten the hook barb with pliers to make removal easy. The fish often needs reviving and you must hold it upright in the water while you move it back and forth, circulating water in its mouth and out its gills.

Other Fish Caught While Fishing for Tarpon. Jack crevalle, snook, shark, redfish, trout, cobia, permit, and barracuda.

Regulations

- Closed Season: none
- Minimum Size: no regulation
- Maximum Size: no regulation
- Daily Bag Limit: two fish may be kept provided the angler has a $50 permit for each, purchased in advance.

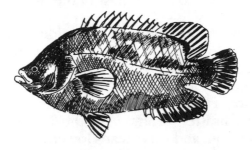

29

Tripletail

(Lobotes surinamensis)

This strong, jumping fish is not as well known as it should be; on light tackle it is a real challenge. They are excellent for eating. All-tackle record: 42 lb 5 oz.

WHERE AND WHEN

1. Entire Gulf coast, but especially from the Ten Thousand Islands to Boca Grande and the Apalachicola Bay area. In the northern part of their range, tripletail are common in the summer; in the southern part, look for them during the winter, November being the peak month.
2. Entire Atlantic coast, especially the Cape Canaveral area. May is the best month.

TACKLE

Spinning and Plug Casting. A rod 5½'-7'; 8#-12# line, mono or braided; spin or conventional reel.

Fly. An 8½'-9' 8-10 weight rod; floating or sink-tip, weight-forward line; a reel holding at least 100 yd 20# Dacron backing.

TECHNIQUES

Spinning and Plug Casting

Live shrimp: Tripletail are nearly always found near some kind of floating or fixed object: navigation markers, pilings, logs, crab and lobster buoys, and weed, even if it is offshore. Pick a day when the water is clear and try to spot fish by cruising near (but not too close) a line of markers or floats in 5'-20' of water. Because tripletail face upcurrent to feed, when you find fish circle and approach them from behind or downcurrent so as neither to disturb the fish nor to drift down upon them. Attach 1' of 20#-40# mono to the line and on the end of that a short-shank 1/0 or 2/0 hook with a live shrimp hooked through the tail. Cast beyond the sighted fish and bring the bait back slowly, right up to the tripletail, and let it sink. Or you can cast upcurrent of a sighted fish and let the tide slowly bring bait and fish together. You can also fish with a float positioned about 18" above the hook. A small crab is another good live bait.

Artificial bait: Proceed the same way as above, but use a yellow or white jig tipped with a piece of shrimp.

Fly. Find fish as previously described and cast a shrimp imitation with brown grizzly feathers, a green and white glass-minnow type streamer, and, on bright days, a brown or black streamer. Set the hook hard on the take.

How to Land a Tripletail. Because of their sharp gill covers, you should use a landing net when bringing in tripletail.

Other Fish Caught While Fishing for Tripletail. Cobia, kingfish, and Spanish mackerel.

Regulations

- Minimum Size: 15" overall
- Maximum Size: no regulation
- Daily Bag Limit: 2

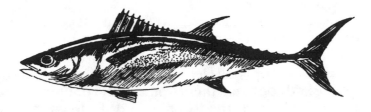

30

Tunas

Their powerful, streamlined bodies make tunas the fastest of all fishes. The following are the common Florida species for which the International Game Fish Association keeps all-tackle records:

- Little tunny (*Euthynnus alletteratus*) 35 lb 2 oz, found in the Atlantic Ocean and the Gulf of Mexico.
- Skipjack (*Euthynnus pelamis*) 45 lb 4 oz, found primarily in the Atlantic Ocean but in the Gulf of Mexico, also.
- Blackfin tuna (*Thunnus atlanticus*) 45 lb 8 oz, found in the Atlantic Ocean and the Gulf of Mexico.
- Yellowfin tuna (*Thunnus albacares*) 388 lb 12 oz, found in the Atlantic Ocean and the Gulf of Mexico.
- Atlantic bonito (*Sarda sarda*) 18 lb 4 oz, found in the Atlantic Ocean but not common in the Gulf of Mexico.

The yellowfin (also called the Allison tuna) and the blackfin are very good to eat. The skipjack is commonly called the Arctic or oceanic bonito and the little tunny is much more often called bonito (confusion would seem to occur with the Atlantic bonito but the latter is not a very common fish). Preferred water temperature: in the seventies.

WHERE AND WHEN

1. Off the Atlantic coast of Florida, especially in the southern part, beginning in the fall and continuing throughout the winter, the little tunny can be caught from as close in as fishing piers to as far out as the "Hump," a sub-ocean mount off Islamorada in the Keys which rises to 240′ from the surface. The blackfin and oceanic bonito can be caught at the same time in the same area but are never as close to shore. Look for them from the reefs out. Yellowfin are caught during the fall and winter also but are usually far out, over the Continental Shelf. In the north, such as off St. Augustine, yellowfin are found in May, September, and October and will come closer to shore when it is very warm. In the north, blackfin are relatively numerous in March along the 28-fathom curve.
2. Along the Gulf coast of Florida, tunas are found mainly in the southern part but in the summer some are caught off the Panhandle. As on the Atlantic coast, bonito come into shallow Gulf water and are caught off passes and beach tide rips.

TACKLE

Trolling. For bonito, blackfin, and oceanic tunas a 20#-30# outfit is correct as this is what you would be using for general trolling. The larger yellowfin demand at least a 50# outfit. Line, rod, and reel are the same as used for any other large ocean fish.

Spinning and Plug Casting. For bonito, blackfin, and oceanic tuna, a 6′-7′ rod; 12#-15# line, mono or braided; conventional reel holding 250-300 yd of line.

Fly. The same as for sailfish, p. 84.

TECHNIQUES

Trolling. Florida tuna are usually caught while trolling for some other fish. However, there are often large schools of bonito and rapidly trolling a spoon or a feather jig close to the edge of the school will pick them up. They will also hit trolled dead bait but artificials are nearly as good. Although bonito like a white or green and yellow jig with Mylar in it, during the summer along the weed rips they go for black feathers, up to 2 oz. Spoons should be kept small: a #1 or #2 Huntington Drone. Blackfin school, also, and the baits above work, but none gets a blackfin's interest as much as a live ballyhoo trolled slowly far astern of the boat, about 125′-150′. Oceanic bonito are usually picked up individually as they are never as numerous as the others. Yellowfin are found as singles or in schools and can be best caught on slowly-trolled large plugs such as the Magnum Rapala; you should go deep with a downrigger, a planer, wire line, or regular line weighted with a trolling lead. Because treble hooks on plugs are not very strong, you cannot pressure a large tuna too much; set the drag light, about 10 lb on a 50# outfit. Yellowfin also hit live mullet slowly trolled; use a strip or ballyhoo with a large feather ahead and trolled to swim, not skip, or a 6″-8″ fast-trolled artificial lure such as those used for blue marlin. Use hooks no smaller than 9/0. If you know yellowfin are in the vicinity, teasers such as those also used for blue marlin should be put out. When a yellowfin strikes, it usually is a hook-up; but if one misses, jig the bait but don't drop back. In fact, flat lines are fine for this fish and outrigger pins should be lowered to your eye level to shorten the drop back. Be on the lookout for schools of porpoise (bottlenose dolphins—the mammal): tuna are often deep beneath them.

Spinning and Plug Casting. When bonito or blackfin are schooling, quietly approach the fringe of the churning water and cast a spoon, jig, or floating plug. Use a short leader of 30# mono.

Fly. Find schooling fish as above and try to get close enough to cast. If you can't, try chumming with cut-up pieces of fish. Station the boat in current that will carry the chum to the tuna school while, at the same time, keep the boat away from it. Use a regular tapered leader that you buy or one such as described for redfish but without a shock as tuna cut-offs are rare. Yellowfin tuna to 81 lb have been taken on a fly rod and for fish of this size, a 16# tippet is certainly necessary. You might, therefore, opt for an 8# tippet for smaller fish such as schooling bonitos and blackfins.

But be aware that a fish with a couple of hundred yards of line out places tremendous strain on the weakest link, the tippet.

This is not the only reason you should use stronger tippets: a tuna you can bring in rapidly is less exhausted and has a better chance of survival when released. With tunas this is more critical than with other fishes because they have a very high oxygen need and because they have no swim bladder, tuna will sink and die unless given extra consideration. For flies, use needlefish imitations in green and white, about 4″ long; the Old Glory streamer; a polar-bear-hair and Mylar streamer; glass minnow imitations; yellow and white Deceivers; and large muddlers. Retrieve in long and rapid strips.

How to Revive a Tuna. On light tackle small tuna that have been on the hook a long time are pretty well beaten down by the time you get them to boatside; note how quickly those you keep die. For this reason, heavier tackle will enable the fisherman to rapidly bring the tuna to the boat. But even then the fish needs help. Tunas have a prominent tail so you can hold the fish just ahead of this fin and your hand won't slip off while you move the fish back and forth in the water. Depending on the fish's condition, this can take five minutes or longer. Continue until the tuna shows some life and seems able to swim off on its own.

Other Fish Caught While Fishing for Tunas. Close-in, as for bonito just off the beach, bluefish, snook, redfish, barracuda, and Spanish mackerel. Far out, as for yellowfin in deep water, you may catch marlin, wahoo, and dolphin.

Regulations (none)

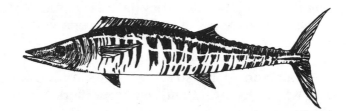

Wahoo; Ocean Barracuda; Tigerfish
(Acanthocybium solanderi)

At a known speed of 50 mph, the wahoo may be one of the fastest fishes in the sea and its first run may burn out a good reel's drag as the fish peels off hundreds of yards of line. They make an excellent meal. Preferred water temperature: 70°–86°F. All-tackle record: 158 lb 8 oz.

WHERE AND WHEN

1. Atlantic coast, especially from the middle of the state and down through the Keys. Some wahoo, however, are caught in the Gulf Stream, 40-50 miles offshore in the spring and summer off St. Augustine and Jacksonville. The best area, south Florida through the Keys, enjoys good wahoo fishing nearly all year. They are generally found as loners outside the reef, in water from 120'-600'.
2. Gulf coast, along the Panhandle in late spring and early summer, at least 20 miles out.

TACKLE

Trolling. 20#-30# outfit, mono or braided line; a 4/0 conventional reel; rod from 5½' stand-up type to a 7' conventional type.

TECHNIQUES

Ocean Trolling

Natural Bait. Most wahoo are caught while fishing for other species such as sailfish and dolphin. Therefore, follow the directions given for these fishes with generally used dead baits such as mullet and ballyhoo which have proven successful. A swimming bait is better than a skipping one when fishing for wahoo. Troll only from flat lines or from an outrigger line whose pin has been lowered to your eye level; dropback must be reduced to a minimum. Some believe trolling mirrored flashing teasers attract wahoo so you might tow a couple from the stern. However, wahoo are usually caught 10'-40' deep and for this reason fishermen after dolphin, for example, often sink a bait to this level to try for wahoo. This can be accomplished with either a trolling lead (8 oz or more), wire line, planer, or a downrigger, the most popular (and expensive) way to fish deep. When using a downrigger, the bait should be 100'-150' behind the lead ball which should be banana-shaped for best results. Attach a stinger hook to a large mullet or a ballyhoo. A ballyhoo needs a skirt and, among other colors, red and black is a good combination. Live bait can also be used on a downrigger. Although wahoo can be found anywhere outside the reef line, fishermen usually expect them at the edge of the blue and green water, near a weed line or debris, and over deep wrecks.

Artificial Bait. A great number of artificial baits may be used to catch wahoo. The hook used must be very sharp and should be attached to 1' of #6-#8 wire. Attach a ball-bearing swivel to the wire's other end with a hay-wire and barrel twist. To the swivel, using an improved clinch knot, tie on 6'-8' of 60#-80# mono and to the end of this attach another ball-bearing swivel. The business end can be a red and black Japanese feather; an Islander Hawaiian Eye lure in yellow and white with a ballyhoo attached or in black and white with a strip bait attached; a Moldcraft Hooker; or, for that matter, any of the fast-trolling lures. Large mackerel-marked plugs, the Boone Cairns Swimmer, the Australian Runner, and the Flashdancer can be trolled and some should be equipped with wire leaders to get a little extra depth.

Spoons are good, too, but must be attached to the wire with a spoon wrap. Try the #3½ Huntington Drone Spoon or a #18 or #19 Acetta Spoon with the blue or red diamond on the face of the spoon. Some fishermen choose spoons for wahoo with great care: a blue-faced spoon for early morning; a chrome spoon for around noon; a red or gold spoon for late afternoon; and, if fishing deep, a blue spoon. Any of these artificials are very effective when fished on a downrigger.

Deep Jigging. Near the same weed line or debris you find for trolling, stop and drift and deep jig with a white jig, about 1 oz-4 oz.

How to Land a Wahoo. This is a powerful fish and long, hard runs are commonplace. Expect the fish to make some spectacular jumps. The boat handler must be very alert because wahoo often charge the boat which must be moved quickly to get away from the fish in order to immediately reduce slack line. At the boat, wahoo often charge beneath, so moving at a rate below trolling speed can prevent this. If a plug with treble hooks is used, leave the fish in the box until it dies before trying to recover it.

Other Fish Caught While Fishing for Wahoo. Sailfish, white marlin, dolphin, and tunas.

Regulations (none)

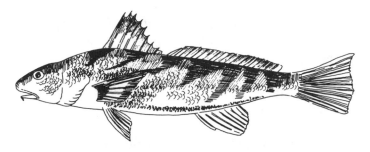

32

Whiting; Sea Mullet; Southern Kingfish
(Menticirbus americanus)

The whiting is a fish commonly caught while fishing in the surf for pompano. The International Game Fish Association keeps no records for whiting but a 2 lb-3 lb fish, a "bull" whiting as they are called, would be a large one, but most are under 1 lb. Although somewhat bony, whiting are considered excellent eating fish. Preferred water temperature: 70°-86° F.

WHERE AND WHEN
Although they are scarce in southeast Florida, whiting are found in the surf and on sandy bay bottoms over the rest of the Florida coast. They are caught all year, but summer and fall are the best times. Whether fishing from a pier or the surf, cast into the sloughs, and fish the last part of the flood tide and the first of the ebb.

TACKLE
The same as for pompano.

TECHNIQUES

Natural Bait. Use sand fleas as described under pompano but try a small hook, about a #4. Whiting also readily bite dead shrimp and clams.

Artificial Bait. Nylon or feather jigs somewhat smaller than used for pompano—⅛ oz - ¼ oz—in yellow, white, or chartreuse bounced along the sandy bottom are effective lures; adding a small sand flea on the jig hook is a good idea. Watch for puffs of sand which sometimes indicate a school of whiting. Use a 1'-2' piece of 20# mono as a leader to guard against a cut-off from other, more toothy fishes.

Fly. About the same as for pompano; use a sinking line and a weighted fly in red and white or black and white.

Other Fish Caught While Fishing for Whiting. Snook, Spanish mackerel, pompano, flounder, catfish, and bluefish.

Regulations (none)

33

Occasional Catches

This book considers the main sport and food fishes in Florida's saltwater, but there are others you will catch while fishing for those listed herein. However, there are a couple more that deserve a few words as some fishermen devote much time to their capture.

TILE FISH

Found all around the state, there are two species of tile fish that are growing in popularity as catching traditional kinds grows more difficult. The gray tile fish (*Caulolatilus microps*) grows to about 2' and is caught in water 240'-780' deep. The golden tile fish (*Lopholatilus chamaeleonticeps*), the better for eating of the two, grows to about 50 lb and is caught in water 250'-1,500' deep, where the temperature ranges from 49°-58° F. Because of these great depths, tile fish are not only difficult to find but are hard work to fish due to the heavy weights or great quantity of wire line used. Electrically-powered reels are standard for the job. Cut bait such as bonito, mullet, menhaden, and squid are used on a 3/0-8/0 hook rig combined with a 300# leader. Also, jigs of about 6 oz or more with a 6"-8" plastic or real fish strip are used.

Regulations (none)

SPEARFISH
(Tetrapturus pfluegeri)

This fish can be distinguished in its group by its relatively short bill. It is rarely caught but a few each season are picked up offshore by those fishing for other billfish.

Regulations

No size regulation but one per day of any billfish.

STRIPED MULLET
(Mugil cephalus)

Particularly along the Gulf coast but also elsewhere, as in the northeast, people use hook and line to fish for the striped mullet, a fish ordinarily taken commercially in nets. Using a long cane pole or a light spinning rod plus 10#-12# clear mono line, a cork float, and strong #6 hooks, mullet are caught particularly during hot summer weather in brackish to fresh water. Bait is a piece of earthworm, about one inch long, but the fish are always first attracted by using chum made of chicken-laying mash straight or mixed with oatmeal or a similar cereal. Not only are mullet good to eat but even an average 1′ fish will put up a very powerful fight.

Regulations

Daily Bag Limit: 50 per boat

BLACK SEA BASS or ROCK BASS
(Centropristis striata)

Caught all along both coasts, this bottom-dweller can be found over wrecks, reefs, or any other kind of bottom structure and also around piers and jetties. It bites all year and is a game little fish that is excellent for eating. Caught generally while fishing for any bottom fish, black sea bass eat any fish, crustacean, or mollusk bait and, in addition, go for 1 oz jigs worked just over the bottom in about 30′ or more water. Preferred water temperature: 55°-68° F. All-tackle record: 9 lb 8 oz.

Regulations

They must be at least 8″ overall.

BROADBILL SWORDFISH
(Xiphias gladius)

This great fighting fish once was the goal of every billfisherman but the small Florida population has been nearly wiped out by commercial long-liners. A few are still caught but it is not considered an important Florida game fish any longer. Generally found in water 120′-600′ deep, fishermen cruise around until a broadbill is spotted on the surface, dorsal and caudal fins sticking prominently out of the water. Then a slowly-trolled squid is pulled right under the great fish's nose. The best fishing is at night when a squid or sometimes a Spanish mackerel is lowered 60′ or so and slowly drifted, an all-night job whether you hook a fish or not. July is considered the best month although any warm weather is good. Preferred water temperature: 58°-70° F. All-tackle record: 1,182 lb.

Regulations (none)

HOGFISH OR HOG SNAPPER
(Lachnolaimus maximus)

Caught primarily on reefs and other structure, this fish reaches 25 lb and is prized for its excellent white flesh. However, as with larger amberjacks and some groupers, the hogfish is suspected of causing ciguatera, the often fatal poisoning one can get from eating certain fishes. They are found mainly along the Atlantic coast and are caught when one fishes for snapper or grouper.

Regulations

- Minimum Size: 12″ from nose to fork in tail
- Maximum Size: no regulation
- Daily Bag Limit: 5

34

Live Bait—
Catching and Keeping

Nearly all fishermen will agree that the use of live bait is simply the best way to catch fish. Although it may be more sporting or more of a challenge to use an artificial lure or to rig a dead bait to look alive, there is no denying that if you can put a live one in a fish's eyesight, your chances of success increase tremendously. And although some live bait can be bought in bait and tackle stores or from bait-catchers on site, when none is available a fisherman has to know how to catch and keep what is needed.

Animals such as crabs that spend part of their time out of water need only to be picked up by hand or net and kept in wet seaweed in a cool place. However, full-time swimmers such as shrimp and fish need much more care. Immediately after catching they must be placed in the same water they came from in an uncrowded condition. Bait containers designed to remain in the water are fine so long as bait has room to breathe when you move the container from one body of water to another. These are primarily designed for shrimp and small fishes.

For larger fishes, sometimes around 12", very large containers such as the biggest plastic garbage containers are necessary. It is always difficult to know how large the container must be; the guiding rule is to use the largest one you can handle so that extra bait caught can be easily kept alive.

But that is not all. A strong aerating pump must be used to oxygenate the water from where you catch the bait to where you intend to use them. And when you have arrived at the boat or shoreline, fresh seawater must be pumped into the container and provision must be made for an efficient overflow, one that will send old water back to the sea, not around your bait.

If the boat has a live bait well, you might want to transfer your catch to it. A few fish in a large well is acceptable but you must consider that water may not circulate when you are under way and, depending on how far away you intend to use the live bait, a pump for the bait well may be necessary. In addition, only a rounded live bait well is acceptable as many fishes need this shape to swim in their customary circular pattern. Many fishermen, for these and other reasons, use a large garbage can or a professionally-made above-deck circular bait tank or tanks even though their boats are equipped with live bait wells.

LIVE BAIT FISH

The following are common live bait fishes used in Florida saltwater and included are their local names. For each there is information about how and where to catch it, and more of this can be found in the book under each species of game fish.

Blue Runner (Hard Tail). Fish in 6'-10' of water over sand where there are dark patches, a rocky bottom, or near navigation markers close to shore. Use a light spinning rod with or without 3' of 20# mono as a leader. Troll and jig the rod tip. Use a 00 Drone or Reflecto spoon with a 1 oz egg sinker ahead of the swivel if they don't bite at the surface. Another effective blue runner bait is one to four white or yellow ⅛ oz jigs tied on 12#-20# mono about 10" apart; these must be jigged rapidly while trolling. To use blue runners, a 3/0-6/0 hook, depending on the size of the bait, should pass through both lips or go through the back just ahead of the dorsal fin and only about ½" deep.

Mullet. Although directions in this book are given on how to catch mullet with hook and line, no one would expect to catch enough for bait this way. Schooling mullet must be located in shallow water along the edge of the Intracoastal Waterway, the beach, or an inlet where you can sneak up to them in a boat and use a cast net. There is a heavy run of mullet along the Atlantic coast in September and October, but some can be found most of the year. Mullet should be hooked through ½″ of flesh ahead of the dorsal fin if fishing in shallow water and through the upper lip if fishing deep. Some people slit the lower lip as they feel it helps the mullet to breathe.

Pilchard (Threadfin Herring, Whitebait, Shiner, Greenie). Find schools before daylight by using a depth finder or anchor near a fishing pier, around a marker near the mouth of an inlet, in the tideline outside an inlet or pass on an ebb tide, or along the beach in 20′-25′ of water. Chum with a ground-up fish mixture and use a light spinning rod with about 8# mono line and no leader. Attach to the line 3 or 4 gold hooks, #8 or #10, about 3″-4″ apart and to the end of the line tie on a ½-1 oz bank sinker. Lower the unbaited hooks to the fish feeding on the chum and jig. In daylight, if pilchards are bunched into a school, use a cast net. Hook pilchards with a 4/0-6/0 under the dorsal fin or just ahead of it when drifting and, if slow-trolling, pass the hook through the eye socket or through both lips.

Bonito (Little Tunny). While trolling offshore in blue or green water, keep a hand line out about 30′; its strength should be sufficient to bring in a bonito quickly. Use a 6′ 40# mono leader and attach a white Japanese feather about 2″ long or a small spoon at the end of it. As soon as you catch bonito, rig it with the eye socket method. Bonito can also be fished alive by hooking them through the upper lip or ahead of the dorsal fin.

Goggle Eye (Bigeye Scad). Found mainly between Jupiter and Fort Lauderdale in 20′-40′ of water, goggle eye can be located with a depth finder. Their usual habitat is near a pier or some such structure. They can be caught the same way as blue runners are caught but you need to troll slowly, jig rapidly, and be out there at 3 a.m. Off Palm Beach, goggle eyes are caught with a dropper rig similar again to the one used for blue runners but with up to a dozen white, yellow, and green quills (unweighted nylon jigs) tied into the fishing line. These are jigged around structure. Rig goggle eyes as with bonito.

Ballyhoo (Balao). Locate schools along the south Florida coast down to the Keys by looking for the fish skipping across the water surface near inlet mouths, outside reefs, or in any offshore water 15′-20′ deep. When fish are located, chum them close with frozen commercial chum, oatmeal, or a mixture of the two. Use a cast net, if possible, but if ballyhoo are not numerous, use a rig as described for pilchards but with lighter line and hooks as small as #16; they should be long-shanked so they can't be swallowed. Bait the hooks with tiny bits of fresh shrimp; a float on the line helps if the wind will carry the bait to the fish. (It is now against the law to use a breakaway, plastic float.) When keeping ballyhoo in a bait well, don't mix them with other kinds of live bait. To use ballyhoo, hook them through the upper lip or follow the instructions in the section on sailfish, p. 86.

Pinfish. Found over a grassy bottom usually near docks and seawalls, pinfish can be chummed and then one can capture them with either a cast net or a beach seine. They can also be caught on a light spinning rod with a rig similar to those already described: a small bank sinker at the end of the fishing line and several #8 or #10 hooks tied above a few inches apart. Bait with tiny pieces of shrimp, little bits of mullet gizzard (it's tough and stays on the hook), or ½″ squares of scaled mullet belly. Hook pinfish ahead of the dorsal fin if there is much current or behind the dorsal if the water is slow-moving.

Needle Fish. Catch at night by hanging a light source over the water at a dock or bridge and capturing the fish with a long-handled dip net. Be careful of their teeth while you hook them with a #2 in the back about the middle of the fish or through the eyes. Freelining them or using a small cork is the way to rig.

Yellowtail. In the Indian River these are used for trout. Catch them under bridges and causeways with a light spinning rod and use #6 treble hooks baited with tiny pieces of shelled shrimp. Add a small split shot weight to get the bait down a bit. Use a #2 hook under the dorsal fin when hooking yellowtail to catch trout.

Pigfish. Used in the Indian River and Mosquito Lagoon areas, catch pigfish in a wire mesh fish trap baited with crushed crab or clams and left out overnight. Try over a grassy bottom in shallow water near channel markers. They can also be caught on small hooks baited with bits of mullet or with a cast net.

Scaled Sardine (Shiner). Used often in the heat of summer when they are easy to catch along the southwest coast, a cast net on inshore grass flats is the standard approach. During the winter, scaled sardines are in deeper channel water near markers and a large, heavy cast net is necessary.

Bull Minnow. Used often in the Panhandle, catch them with a minnow trap in grassy sloughs inside bays and harbors. Use a ball of bread dough as bait and leave it out overnight. If you see bull minnows in a tidal pool, use a cast net or beach seine. Hook them through the lips.

Spot. Considered in Jupiter as one of the best snook baits, catch them by cast netting in the surf on the south side of the south jetty or with a light spinning rod using small hooks and bits of fresh shrimp on the patch reefs north of Jupiter Inlet.

Menhaden (Bunker, Shad, Leroy, LY). On both coasts of north Florida, menhaden are caught while schooling in the surf; use a cast net.

Glass Minnow. Using a small mesh cast net, these can be found in boat basins and residential canals.

Mojarra (Mutton Minnow, Shad, Sand Bream). Found on grassy, sandy, and other such open sea bottom and at the edge of the surf line, mojarras are caught with cast net or beach seine.

Speedo. Considered good live bait for amberjack, catch them in the Keys by chumming over a shallow reef and use pieces of bonito as bait. December through April is the best time.

Snappers, Grunts, etc. These reef and shallow water fishes are caught as explained in appropriate sections in this book. They are all good live bait and should be hooked ahead of the dorsal fin or through the lips.

GAME FISHES AND THEIR FAVORITE LIVE BAIT

- Amberjack: speedo, blue runner
- Barracuda: all fishes up to one or two pounds
- Bluefish: Any fish up to a pound
- Blue Marlin: bonito (little tunny), school dolphin
- Bonefish: crab, shrimp
- Cero Mackerel: ballyhoo
- Cobia: grunts, pinfish, blue runner, catfish, large shrimp, sardine, silver trout, small blue crab, eel, menhaden
- Dolphin: mullet, grunts
- Drum: blue crab, fiddler crab, sand flea, pinfish, shrimp
- Flounder: mullet, bull minnow
- Groupers: any small fish
- Grunts: glass minnow
- Jacks: menhaden, mullet, any small fish
- Kingfish: grunt, yellowtail snapper, mullet, shrimp
- Ladyfish: sand fleas, shrimp
- Permit: blue crabs, fiddler crabs, shrimp
- Pompano: sand fleas, clams, shrimp
- Redfish: shrimp, crab, pinfish, pigfish
- Sailfish: mullet, ballyhoo, goggle eye
- Seatrout: shrimp, mullet, yellowtail (not the snapper), pigfish, pinfish, needle fish
- Sharks: any fish, the size depending upon the shark
- Sheepshead: fiddler crabs, other crabs, shrimp, sand fleas, clams, tube worm
- Snappers: glass minnows, pinfish
- Snook: shrimp, mullet, pinfish, greenies, menhaden, Spanish sardines, cigar minnows, goggle eye
- Spanish Mackerel: glass minnows, pilchard, shrimp, ballyhoo, sardine, whitebait
- Striped Bass: eel, shiner
- Tarpon: shrimp, pilchard, mullet, pinfish, crab, shiners, sand perch, blue runner
- Tripletail: shrimp, crab

- Tunas: any small fish up to a few pounds
- Wahoo: blue runner, mullet
- White Marlin: mullet, ballyhoo, goggle eye
- Whiting: sand fleas, shrimp

35

Chumming

Whenever you fish from a more or less stationary position, it is necessary to try to bring the fish to you. Chumming is a method that can be done anywhere: the surf, inlets, bays, deep sea, over reefs, wrecks, etc. Some control is important as the goal is to attract fish, not to feed them, so consideration of how to chum properly is in order.

There are a few rules:

1. Fresh chum is better than frozen.
2. When using frozen chum, place it in a container such as a bucket with holes punched in it or a small-mesh bag.
3. The chum container can be tied so it releases on the surface or weighted so you can chum at any chosen depth.
4. When not using a chum container, mix chum with sand as it helps it to sink.
5. Also when not using a chum container, you must chum frequently: fish are only interested when there is an unbroken line of chum.
6. Chum is not only ground-up fish, shrimp, etc. but can be chunks of fish or shrimp or even the whole animal; chum-

ming whole dead glass minnows and whole live pilchards
are examples.
7. Chum is more effective when made from an oily fish.
8. Sometimes only fish oil—such as from menhaden—makes
good chum.
9. The relatively new saltwater fish attractants can be used as
chum.

Any kind of sea life you would use as bait can be chum, but also
some canned foods work. Here is a list of various chum:

1. Shrimp, shrimp heads and pieces cut up, ground up, or diced.
2. Clams, cut up or ground up, and also their shells whole or
broken up.
3. Barnacles, ground up or crushed.
4. Oysters, ground up or crushed.
5. Fish blood.
6. Any fish part, ground up.
7. Live or dead whole fishes.
8. Any of the throw-away sea life commercial shrimp boats
catch in their nets.
9. Canned jack mackerel mixed with a loaf of white bread
plus enough sea water to make it a paste.
10. Canned cat food mixed with bread plus sea water.
11. Dry seafood-flavored cat food.
12. A mixture of dry and canned cat food plus water and frozen
in plastic bags.
13. Cooked elbow macaroni to which a little fish oil or fish
attractant has been added.
14. Oatmeal straight from the box or mixed with any of the
above.
15. Blood and slaughter-house animal parts for sharks.

Knots and Wire Connections

There are truly hundreds of fishing line knots one could learn, but the following few are all you need to know to fish following the directions in this book.

IMPROVED CLINCH KNOT

Use to attach any kind of fishing line to a hook eye, swivel, or artificial lure.

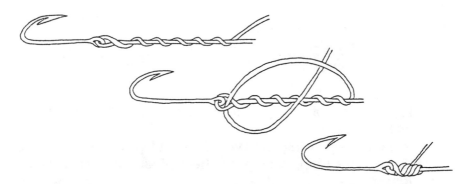

1. Thread the line through the hook eye (or whatever) and pull out about four or more inches of it.
2. Wrap this end around the main, longer line five turns or turn the hook five times.

3. Put the end through the space between the hook eye and the first fishing line wrap.
4. Bring the end back through the loop just formed in step 3 and pull it through just enough so that it will not fall back out.
5. Wet the line making up the knot, hold on to the hook, and pull on the longer line while at the same time keeping the short line end taut—you may need to push the knot towards the hook eye.
6. When the knot pulls up and is tight, trim off the end.

DOUBLE SURGEON'S KNOT

Use to attach two pieces of mono or any other material when one is no more than five times as heavy as the other.

1. Lay two ends of line opposite each other, overlapping six to eight inches.
2. Make a loop using the two lines and pass the free end through the loop, making sure both pieces of line are used.
3. Repeat.
4. Wet the line making up the knot and, tightly holding the two pieces of line on either side, slowly and steadily pull to tighten the knot—tighten again by pulling the individual strands.
5. Trim the ends.

DOUBLE SURGEON'S LOOP

Use to form a loop to connect with another loop or for making rigs such as for pompano, grouper, and snapper.

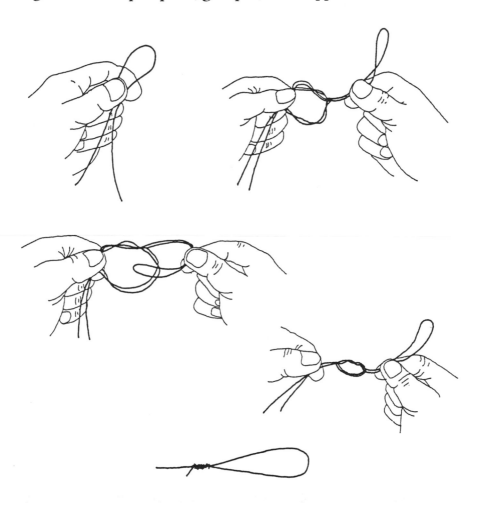

1. Double the line to form a long, flat loop, make a loop in the doubled line as above, and pass the closed loop end through two times, just as in the previous knot.
2. After adjusting the loop size and wetting the line forming the knot, pull slowly on both ends to draw it up tight— tighten again by pulling the individual strands.
3. Trim the end.

DOUBLE SURGEON'S LOOP WITH AN ARTIFICIAL LURE

This is an alternative to the improved clinch knot as this one allows the lure more freedom to move.

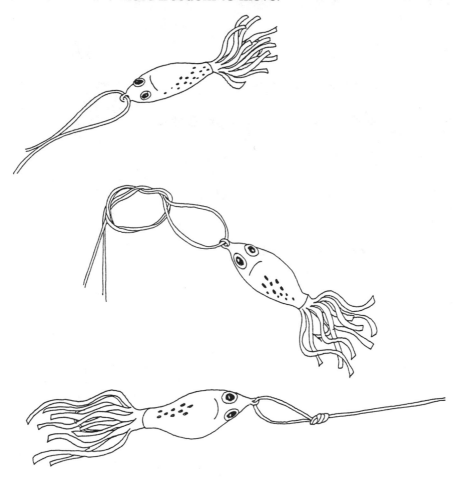

1. Thread the end of the fishing line or leader through the eye of the lure and double it back far enough so that when you make a loop as in the previous knot it will be large enough to accommodate the lure.
2. Proceed as above, this time passing the lure twice through the double line loop.
3. Adjust the loop size, wet the knot, pull up tight, and trim the end.

ALBRIGHT SPECIAL KNOT

Use to attach two pieces of mono or any other material when one is more than five times as heavy as the other—also to attach mono to wire as in the cases of a short tooth-proof shock leader or wire trolling line to backing.

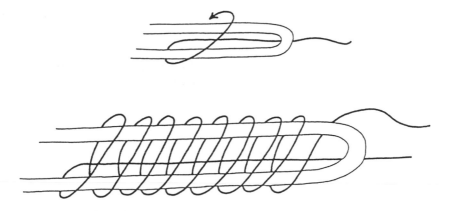

1. Bend back the heavier line so that it lies against itself about four inches or more.
2. With about twelve inches available of the lighter line, lay the end portion of it along the flat loop formed in step 1. (With a Bimini Twist this lighter line can be doubled for added strength and then tied according to these same directions.)
3. Wrap the end portion of the light line around the flat loop beginning at the open end—you will, therefore, be wrapping the light line around itself and the two strands of heavier line and be moving towards the loop—you must wrap with one hand and hold the formed loops between the thumb and first finger of the other hand in an attempt to keep the wraps in place and to prevent them from overlapping.
4. Make at least twelve turns and, when finished, insert the remaining end of the light line back through the same side of the loop as the rest of the light line.
5. Applying tension to both strands of the light line, gradually pull the wrappings (push with your fingers at the same

time) towards the loop bend without allowing them to overlap.

6. Increase pulling pressure by alternately pulling on the short end and then the longer part of the light line until the knot is snug against the loop.
7. Finish by holding on to both light lines while snugging down on the heavy line.
8. Trim the ends.
9. When attaching mono to braided line, make the loop in the mono and wrap the braided around it.
10. When attaching mono to wire, make the loop in the wire and close it with the usual haywire twist and barrel wrap and then flatten it as you will wind the mono around it — some fishermen, when making this splice, finish the mono wrap by passing the end to the other side of the wire loop so that wire ends up between two strands of mono.

BIMINI TWIST

Use to form a long or short loop in the line's end to insure against line fray and to help in boating a fish.

1. You can tie a short Bimini by yourself — longer ones as for ocean trolling are more easily handled by two people.
2. Double back about three feet or more fishing line and hold the two pieces in one hand and insert the other hand into the loop formed.
3. Hold your arms out straight and turn the loop hand twenty times to form twenty long twists in the two pieces of line.
4. Sit down and hold the loop by passing it around your bent knee — maintain pressure on the loop with each hand holding one piece of line.
5. Separate the two lines until they form a right angle with each other and pull towards you until the twists tighten and move towards your knee.
6. While continuing to maintain pressure, shift your hands so that the long part of the line is lined up with the twisted part and the short end is at a right angle to it.

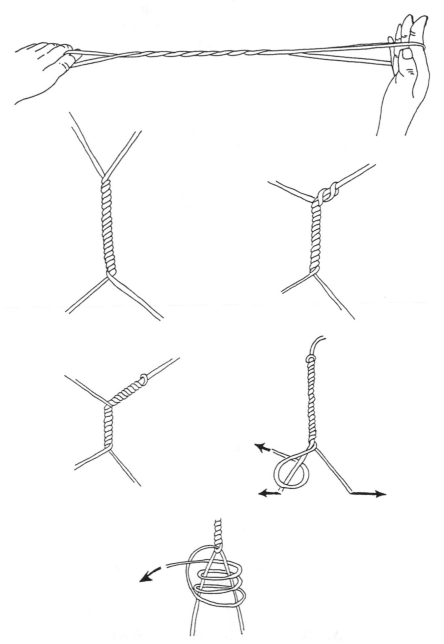

7. Continue to maintain pressure on the longer line and relax a bit on the shorter — if you do this correctly, the short line will roll over the twists in a tight wrap until it reaches the loop.

8. Hold this knot in place and make a half-hitch around one leg of the loop close to the knot and tighten it—do the same to the other leg of the loop.
9. Remove the loop from your knee and place it around a toe or any object that will flatten it.
10. Wrap the end around the two strands about six times (beginning away from the knot and moving towards it) and snug it tightly, and secure with a half-hitch.
11. A Bimini can be tied to a leader or anything else by following the directions for tying a single strand.

FIGURE 8 KNOT

Use to attach light cable or nylon-covered cable to an artificial lure, a swivel, or a hook.

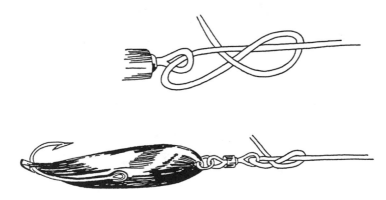

1. Thread the cable through the eye of a hook or lure and wrap it once around itself.
2. Come back around with this end and pass through the formed opening and pull tight with pliers, if necessary, and trim the end.

HAYWIRE TWIST AND BARREL WRAP

For making a loop in single-strand wire or attaching it to a hook or a swivel.

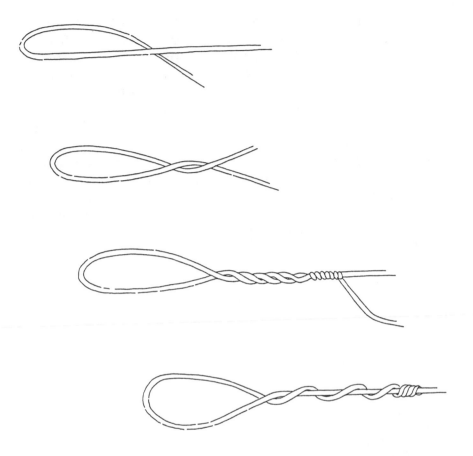

1. Start by using #7 or #8 wire as it is easier to learn with than lighter or heavier wire.
2. Pass about six inches of wire through a hook eye or make a loop with it—what follows is identical in both cases.
3. With the thumb and first finger of one hand hold tightly at the point where the two wires cross.
4. With the other hand, wrap each piece of wire around the other, *not one around the other*—to do this you will need to practice and the illustration shows how it must look after four or five wraps have been made (just as haywire is wrapped.).
5. Now begin the barrel wrap by tightly wrapping the short piece around the longer piece about three or four turns—these wraps should be as close to each other as possible.

6. You should have a two to three inch piece of wire to end up with (if you clip this off with side-cutting pliers it leaves a short spur of wire which cuts hands quickly)—with your thumb push this piece of wire standing out at a right angle down and along the wraps already made—there is no need for it to lie flat, only its angle needs changing.
7. About mid-way in the end piece of wire make a right-angle bend to use as a "crank handle."
8. Crank this handle in a circular motion towards the wire loop or hook eye—you may have to move it back and forth in the beginning but, in any event, move it parallel to the wire wrap, not around it. The break that results will be flush with no projecting sharp end.

SPOON WRAP

Unless you use this attachment when trolling a spoon on a wire leader, the loop will flatten and inhibit the action of the spoon.

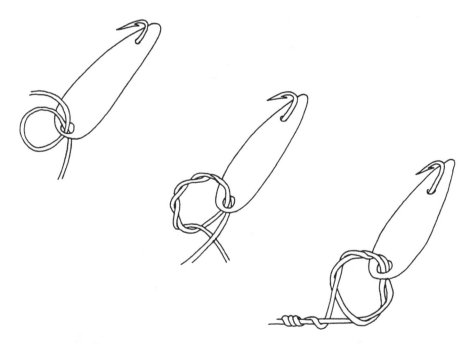

1. Thread the leader wire through the eye of the spoon and pull through a few inches of wire.

2. Pass the leader wire end through the spoon eye again and adjust the formed circle into the size desired.
3. Pass the leader wire around the circle, in and out of the wire at least four wraps, until you come to the beginning.
4. Finish with a haywire twist and a barrel wrap, breaking off the end.

Fishing Rigs

Because these rigs can be used for fishes of various sizes, see the text for the proper leaders, weights, and hooks to use for each fish discussed.

GUPPY RIG

1. Attach the weight and a black swivel to the leader with improved clinch knots.
2. Make two or three short loops in the leader with double surgeon's loops.
3. Pass each loop through the eye of a hook and then around the entire hook and pull up tight.
4. Attach the fishing line to the swivel with an improved clinch knot.

REGULAR BOTTOM RIG

1. Attach the weight and swivel as with the guppy rig.
2. With a double surgeon's loop, make a large loop in the leader about halfway between the weight and swivel.
3. Cut one leg of this loop near the knot to form a long piece of line.

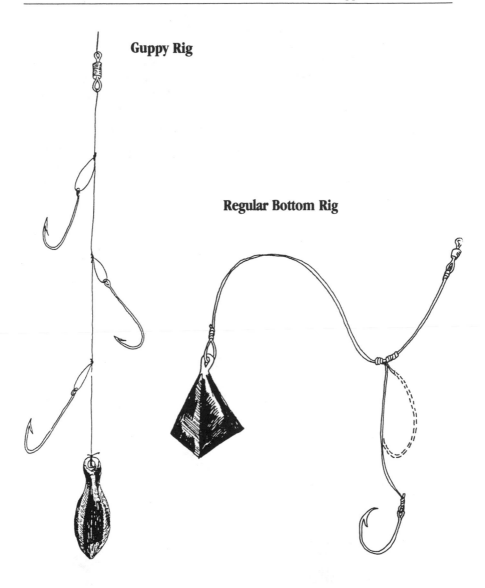

Guppy Rig

Regular Bottom Rig

4. With an improved clinch knot, attach a hook to the end of this piece of line.
5. With the same knot attach the fishing line to the swivel.

FISH FINDER RIG

1. Thread an egg sinker on the fishing line.
2. With improved clinch knots, attach a swivel to the fishing line beneath the sinker, a leader to the other swivel ring, and a hook to the end of the leader.
3. An adaptation of this rig that restricts the free movement of the bait but adds another hook is to tie a surgeon's loop in the line above the weight similar to the guppy rig—if the knot is smaller than the hole in the egg sinker, a bead or a button can be placed above it.

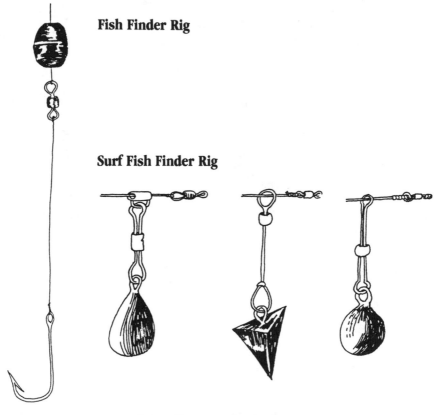

Fish Finder Rig

Surf Fish Finder Rig

SURF FISH FINDER RIG

1. Insert the fishing line through a sliding fish finder device and to it attach a pyramid sinker.

2. Attach a swivel to the end of the fishing line and to the leader, both with improved clinch knots.
3. Attach a hook to the end of the leader with an improved clinch knot.

BREAKAWAY RIG

1. Make up a fish finder rig without the egg sinker.
2. Through an egg sinker, thread either light mono or light copper wire and attach one end above and the other below the swivel—the mono can be lightly tied and the wire simply wrapped around.

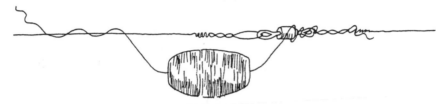

3. Another breakaway rig can be made from a 3-way swivel— tie the fishing line to one ring, a piece of mono and a hook to another, and light mono and a sinker to the third—use improved clinch knots.

FIXED FLOAT RIG

1. Thread a float on the fishing line and fix its position with the peg provided or in any other way depending on the kind of float used.
2. Below the float attach a rig just like the fish finder but without the egg sinker.

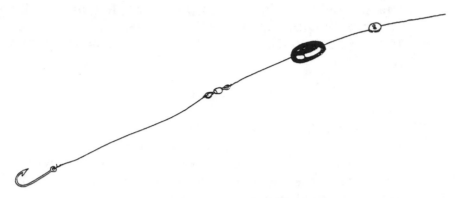

SLIDING FLOAT RIG

1. Tie any knot in the fishing line so that below it the line plus the leader will equal the depth you wish to fish.
2. Thread on the fishing line a small bead (buy in fishing tackle store) or button that will not pass the knot.
3. Thread the float on the fishing line.
4. Below the float attach a rig just like the fish finder but without the egg sinker.

POPPING CORK RIG

1. With a popping cork make up a fixed float rig.
2. If you use an unweighted popping cork you must attach a split shot weight halfway between the cork and hook—a weighted popping cork requires no additional weight.

POMPANO RIG

1. Make up a rig similar to the guppy rig but with four or more hooks and to the end of the leader attach a pyramid sinker.

TEXAS WORM RIG

1. Thread a worm weight (its size depending upon the rod and line size you are using) on the fishing line, pointed end towards the rod tip.
2. Bend a hook slightly back just below its eye.
3. Attach the fishing line to the hook with an improved clinch knot.
4. Work the hook point into the head of a plastic grub or worm until the hook bend is inside and then push the point out.
5. Work the worm or grub head up the hook until it covers the eye and rests against the cup face of the worm weight.

Pompano Rig   **Texas Worm Rig**

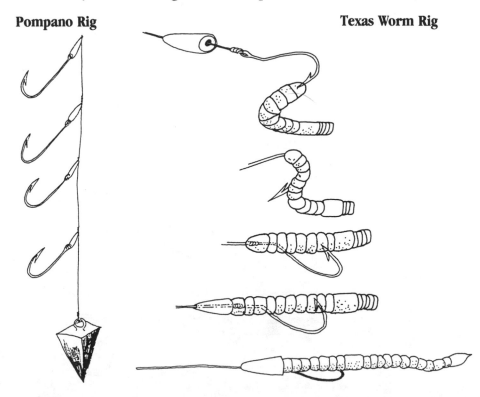

6. Twist the hook around and bury the point and barb in the worm body.
7. The worm weight can be held in place by pushing a round toothpick in the hole at the pointed end and breaking it off.

BALLYHOO TROLLING RIG

1. Using a needle-eye hook, attach wire to the eye with a haywire twist and a barrel wrap, leaving a piece about one

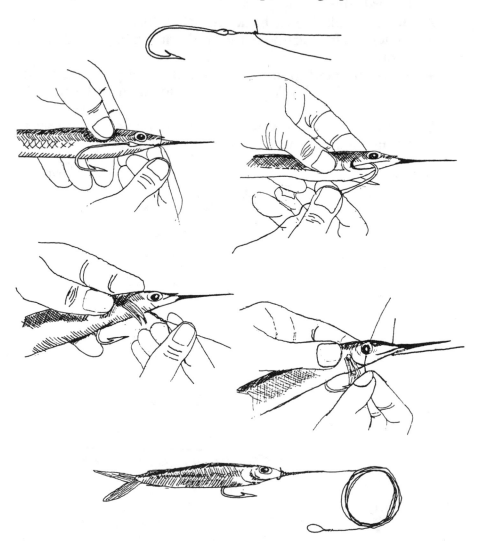

inch long instead of breaking it off—this short wire should stick out at a right angle to the wrappings and be pointed opposite to the hook point.

2. Attach a six inch piece of soft copper rigging wire by wrapping a bit of it around the twisted wire.

3. Choose a ballyhoo of a size so that when you lay the rig above and over it the one inch piece of wire will be in line with a point just behind the tip of the upper jaw—the hook bend should overlay a point in the belly about one-third of the way back of the head (in the future, the rig size can be adjusted to bait size).

4. Open a gill cover and insert the hook point and work the hook back through and inside the body—let it emerge from the belly so that the upright piece of wire is lined up with the jaws—the hook eye and twisted wire should be behind and inside the gill covers.

5. Push the piece of upright leader wire up through the lower and upper jaws—it should emerge through a bony part of the head.

6. Push the end of the piece of copper rigging wire through the ballyhoo's eyes and pull it through—then wrap it around the head once behind and then in front of the protruding piece of leader wire until there is no more to wrap.

7. Break off the bait's bill as close as possible without tearing the lower jaw.

8. With a sharp knife make small slits in the ballyhoo's belly ahead of and behind the bend of the hook so that it will not bind.

9. Although six to nine feet of coffee-stained stainless steel wire has traditionally been used in the regular ballyhoo rig, more bait action can be obtained by using only eight to twelve inches of wire which is then attached to a six to nine foot mono leader. Attach a snap swivel to the end of the leader with an improved clinch knot and make a loop in the short piece of ballyhoo-rigged wire with the usual haywire twist and barrel wrap. Besides the advantages of a more freely-moving bait, ballyhoo rigged this way ahead of time can be stored in ice, ready to be attached to the snap swivel for quick use.

BALLYHOO RIGGED WITH A SKIRT OR FEATHER

1. Before rigging a ballyhoo as explained above, thread a plastic skirt or, to fish a little deeper or to keep the bait from skipping in rough seas, a Japanese feather on the leader wire. Let the plastic skirt or the feather slide back and cover about two-thirds of the ballyhoo's body—this rig not only makes the bait more attractive but relatively weedless, as well.

Ballyhoo Rigged with a Skirt

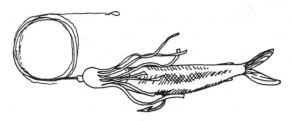

STINGER RIG

1. Used with any bait, live or dead, hooks can be placed as in the illustration. Attach one to another with pieces of leader wire, swivels, or by opening the hook eye with pliers and then squeezing it closed over the bend of another hook.
2. The last stinger can swing free or be imbedded in the bait.
3. You may add a stinger to a hook already in place.

Stinger Rig

MULLET TROLLING RIG

1. Very fresh and firm silver (white) mullet up to ten inches long make the best trolling bait.
2. Remove the backbone with a special aluminum de-boner or with a sharp knife cut along both sides of the backbone

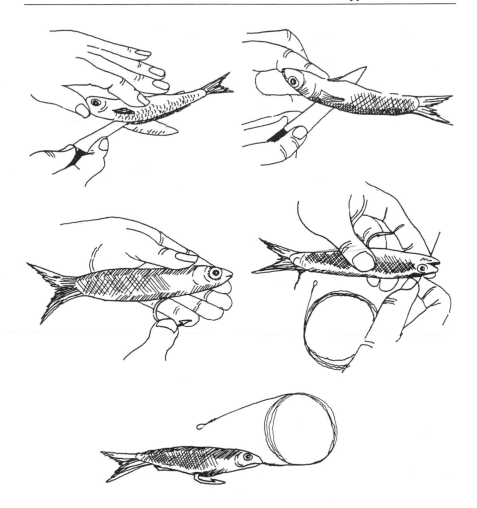

beginning behind the end of the gill cover to just behind the second dorsal fin.

3. Break off the exposed backbone and remove it and the exposed intestines from the slit made in the top of the mullet.
4. With the point of the knife make a very small slit just behind the pelvic fins.
5. Insert the circular eye of a hook into the slit and slide it towards the head until the hook eye is between the mullet's eyes.
6. Push a piece of leader wire (or first make a hole with an ice pick) through the soft spot on the mullet's head down

through and out the underside of the fish—pull and push the hook slightly to make certain the leader has passed through its eye.

7. Curve the end of the wire forward and around the leader, fasten with the haywire twist and barrel wrap, and break off the excess wire. Make certain that the haywire twist begins close to the mullet's mouth so the mouth will not open while trolling.

8. To flatten the mullet's head so it will troll better, tightly tie a piece of string around the head just behind the eyes.

9. To make a mullet rig that will stay down in choppy seas, thread the leader wire through a one-quarter to one ounce egg sinker (depending on the size of the mullet) before making the haywire twist—the weight should be snug against the bait's mouth.

10. As with a ballyhoo, the mullet rig can be made on a short piece of leader wire and fished with a skirt.

STRIP TROLLING RIG

1. Attach leader wire and hook as described for a ballyhoo but leave a three inch piece of wire after the barrel wrap.

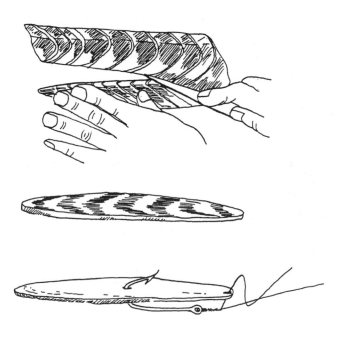

2. With this piece, make a safety pin rig as in the illustration.
3. Use an entire fillet from an eight to twelve inch mullet or a similar piece from a dolphin or bonito belly.
4. While the fillet is held on a cutting board with an ice pick, with a sharp knife shave the excess flesh away from the skin until the remaining piece is about one-eighth inch thick.
5. Cut through the skin to form a piece shaped as in the illustration.
6. If the edges are ragged, bevel them—make the tail pointed and the front end square. The meat side should show muscle fibers pointed towards the tail end of the strip.
7. Lay the safety pin rig on top of the meat side of the strip so that you can tell where the hook must be inserted in order for the safety pin to attach at the front end.
8. Attach and fasten wire as in the illustration.
9. A string tied tightly around the front of the strip just behind the upright piece of wire will help secure the bait.
10. If the strip is long enough, a stinger can be attached— plastic skirts are excellent with strip baits.

LIVE BAIT

1. Attach a hook to a mono leader with an improved clinch knot or to leader wire with the haywire twist and barrel wrap, breaking the wire off flush.

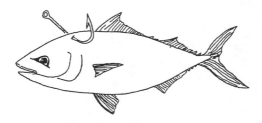

2. As in the illustration, pass the hook under a little flesh just in front of the dorsal fin. Other hook placement is discussed under specific fish chapters.

LIVE BAIT: HEAD BRIDLE

1. First place the bait fish just caught in a wet towel belly-up; it can be held by one person while another attaches the hook. Running saltwater through a hose into the fish's mouth helps.
2. Next find the eye socket, a small passageway through the head. If you look at the right side of the fish's head, you will see this cavity in the one o'clock position relative to the eye; from the left side it appears in the eleven o'clock position.
3. Tie, using any knot, the middle of a 10" piece of 50# Dacron to the bend of a 10/0-14/0 marlin hook that has already been connected by crimping to a 300# mono leader.
4. Then, with an open-eyed rigging needle attached to one end of the line, pass it all the way through the eye socket.
5. Position the hook so that the shank points straight ahead of the bait with the bend between the eyes and the point straight up.
6. Tie the two ends of Dacron to secure the hook to the head. All this should take only a few seconds to ensure that the bait will be lively when put into the water. This is possible by practicing with dead bait and making certain everything is ready when a bait fish is caught.

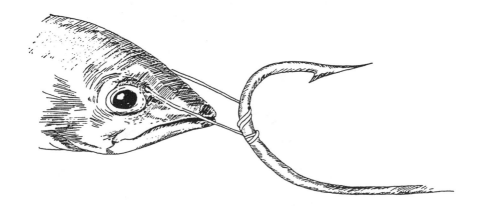

Where to Fish

Fish	NE	NW	mid-E	mid-W	SE	SW	Keys	mangroves	inlet	offshore	inshore	surf
Amberjack**		✕			✕		✕			✕		
Barracuda*			✕	✕	✕	✕	✕		✕		✕	
Bluefish*	✕	✕	✕	✕	✕	✕			✕		✕	✕
Blue marlin**		✕			✕		✕			✕		
Bonefish*							✕	✕			✕	
Cero mackerel**					✕		✕		✕			
Cobia*		✕	✕	✕	✕		✕		✕		✕	
Dolphin**					✕		✕			✕		
Drum	✕	✕	✕	✕					✕		✕	
Flounders	✕	✕	✕	✕					✕		✕	
Groupers*		✕	✕	✕	✕	✕	✕	✕		✕	✕	
Grunts*					✕	✕	✕			✕	✕	
Jacks	✕	✕	✕	✕	✕	✕	✕	✕	✕		✕	✕
Kingfish**	✕	✕	✕	✕	✕	✕	✕			✕		
Ladyfish					✕	✕	✕	✕	✕		✕	
Permit*							✕	✕	✕		✕	
Pompano		✕	✕	✕	✕				✕		✕	
Redfish*	✕	✕	✕	✕		✕		✕	✕		✕	✕
Sailfish**					✕		✕			✕		
Seatrout*	✕	✕	✕	✕		✕	✕	✕	✕		✕	
Sharks*					✕	✕	✕		✕	✕	✕	
Sheepshead	✕	✕	✕	✕	✕	✕		✕	✕		✕	✕
Snappers*		✕	✕	✕	✕	✕	✕	✕	✕	✕	✕	
Snook*			✕	✕	✕	✕	✕	✕	✕		✕	✕
Sp. mackerel*	✕	✕	✕	✕	✕	✕	✕			✕	✕	✕
Striped bass*	✕	✕									✕	
Tarpon*			✕	✕	✕	✕	✕	✕			✕	✕
Tripletail*	✕	✕	✕	✕	✕	✕					✕	
Tunas**					✕		✕			✕		
Wahoo**	✕	✕	✕		✕		✕			✕		
White marlin**		✕			✕		✕					
Whiting	✕	✕	✕	✕							✕	✕

*Boat a help   **Boat necessary

Specific Lures for Certain Fishes

Note: Experimenting will surely demonstrate that the lures below can be successful with more fishes than indicated.

SPOONS

- Reflecto: redfish
- Johnson: redfish, seatrout
- Huntington Drone: tuna, wahoo, kingfish
- Acetta: grouper, redfish, wahoo
- Hopkins: bluefish, tarpon
- Krocodile: bluefish, snook, tarpon
- Gator: bluefish, snook, tarpon
- Sprite: redfish
- Clark: cero mackerel, Spanish mackerel
- Squid: cero mackerel
- Barracuda: redfish

CASTING LURES

- See-Bee: redfish, seatrout
- Maverick: seatrout, snook
- Devil Horse: seatrout
- Tube lure: barracuda

- Dolphin Jr.: dolphin
- Bill Smith Lure: tarpon
- Rag Mop: bluefish
- Boone Needlefish: seatrout
- Atom 40: redfish
- Atom Jr.: redfish
- Gibbs: redfish
- Nickelure Popeye: bonefish, permit
- Gaines Wiggle Jig: bonefish
- Cisco Kid: snook, tarpon, grouper
- Cotee Glitter Shad: seatrout, flounder
- Cotee Liv' Eye Jig: tarpon
- Cotee Grub: redfish
- Bagley Mullet: redfish, seatrout, snook, tarpon
- Bagley Bangolure: striped bass
- Bagley Chugolure: seatrout
- Trader Bay Snook Slayer: snook
- Rebel Jawbreaker: grouper, kingfish
- Rebel Redfin: bluefish, dolphin, snook
- Rebel Jumpin' Minnow: seatrout
- Bomber A Magnum: snook, striped bass
- Bomber Rip Shad: seatrout
- Bomber 16 & 17 series: snook, kingfish
- Creek Chub Darter: seatrout, redfish
- Creek Chub Wiggle Diver: tarpon
- Cordell Spot: redfish
- Cordell Crazy Shad: seatrout
- Rapala Shad Rap: striped bass
- Rapala Magnum: dolphin, grouper, kingfish, redfish, snook, tarpon, tuna
- Rapala CD-9 & CD-14: kingfish, tuna
- Tarpon Taker Jig: tarpon
- Sassy Shad: seatrout
- Burke Top-Dog: seatrout
- Burke Flex-O-Plug: dolphin
- Burke Hookworm: bonefish, redfish
- Rat-L-Trap: grouper, redfish, snook
- Boone Spinana & Castana: redfish, snook
- Zara-types: bluefish, dolphin, seatrout, snook
- Pete's Ling Jig: cobia

- No Alibi Jig: cobia, dolphin
- Red Tailed Hawk: snook
- Mirrolure TT & 7M: redfish, seatrout, snook
- Mirrolure 12M: redfish
- Mirrolure 52M: redfish, seatrout, snook, tarpon
- Mirrolure 60M, 65M, 67M: tarpon
- Mirrolure 72M, 82M, 98MR: snook
- Mirrolure 77M: bluefish
- Mirrolure 85M: snook, tarpon
- Mirrolure 95MR: barracuda, Spanish mackerel
- Mirrolure 111MR: grouper

TROLLING LURES

- Boone Cairns Swimmer: grouper, kingfish, wahoo
- Islander Hawaiian Eye: billfish, wahoo
- Moldcraft Hooker: billfish, wahoo
- Australian Runner: wahoo
- Flashdancer: wahoo
- Sea Witch: dolphin, billfish
- Boone Airhead: billfish
- Arbogast Reto Rig: billfish
- Iland: billfish
- Konahead: billfish
- C & H: billfish
- Schneider: billfish

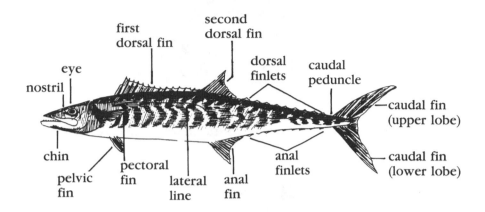

first
dorsal fin

second
dorsal fin

eye

nostril

dorsal
finlets

caudal
peduncle

caudal fin
(upper lobe)

chin

pectoral
fin

anal
finlets

caudal fin
(lower lobe)

pelvic
fin

lateral
line

anal
fin

Identification

This is not intended to be a handbook on identification, but pointing out a few characteristics to look for may help you to know which kind of fish you have caught. The first fifteen fishes listed are easy to recognize because they resemble no other. The next section, starting with the black drum, look like at least one other fish, and the remainder (flounders, snappers, groupers, etc.) are members of large groups of look-alikes and are more difficult to identify.

The Easy Ones and What to Look For

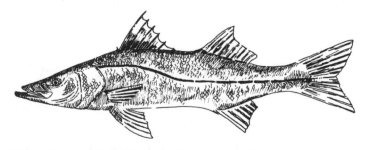

Snook: pugnacious mouth and black body stripe.

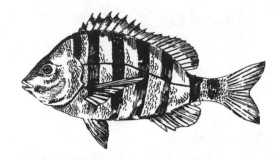

Sheepshead: Sloping forehead and black, nearly vertical bars on body.

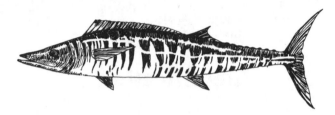

Wahoo: beaklike mouth and vertical bars on body.

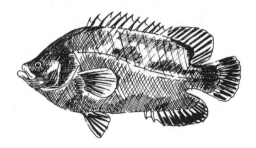

Tripletail: concave forehead, dorsal and anal fins reaching far back.

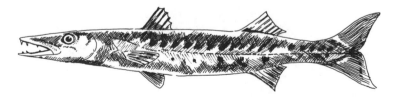

Barracuda: long jaws, large pointed teeth, and dorsal fins far apart.

Dolphin: highly colorful, steep forehead in male, rounded in female.

Cobia: flatish head and stripe down side.

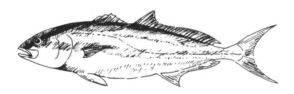

Amberjack: stripe from tip of snout to beginning of dorsal fin.

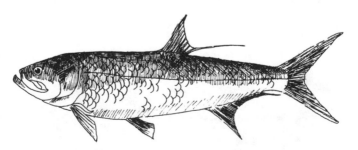

Tarpon: large mouth, protruding lower lip, and enormous scales.

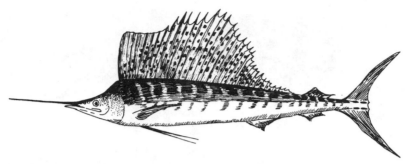

Sailfish: sail-like dorsal fin.

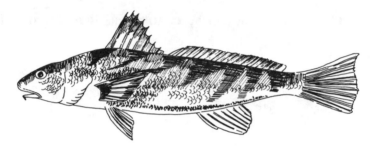

Whiting: barbels under chin.

Striped Bass: seven or eight horizontal black stripes.

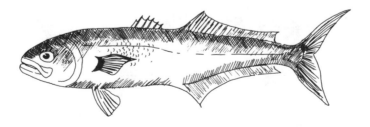

Bluefish: large mouth and teeth, blotch at pectoral fin base.

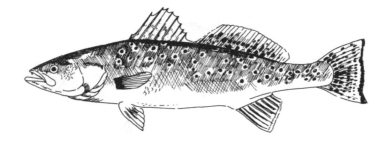

Seatrout: large black spots on upper back, second dorsal and caudal fins. The weakfish is easily distinguished from the seatrout by its lack of spots on the second dorsal fin.

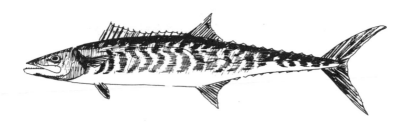

King mackerel: blue back, silvery belly, and a lateral line that drops sharply below the second dorsal fin.

Look-Alikes and What to Look For

Black drum: four or five wide, vertical body bars and chin barbels.

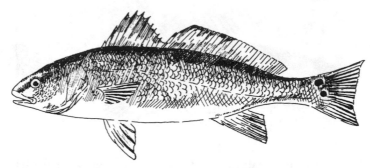

Redfish: bronze body and, often, a black spot or spots near base of caudal fin.

Bonefish: downturned mouth with blackish tip of snout.

Ladyfish: upturned mouth and dorsal fin beginning above a point behind the pelvic fin.

Permit: body more rounded and deeper than pompano.

Pompano: longer, more streamlined than the permit. To distinguish pompano and permit from look-alike jacks, note the hard ridge on the jacks' caudal peduncle, absent on pompano and permit.

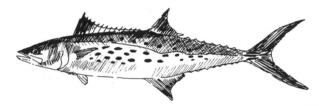

Spanish mackerel: large, yellowish spots on body.

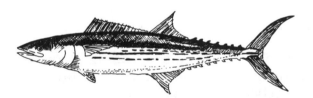

Cero mackerel: short, yellowish streaks on body.

Blue marlin: first dorsal and anal fins rather pointed.

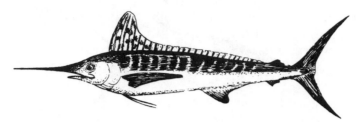

White marlin: first dorsal and anal fins rounded.

The Confusing Groups and What to Look For

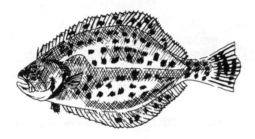

Flounders

Southern flounder: black spots on back in no particular pattern.

Summer flounder: many spots but five large brown ones in rear half of body—one on the lateral line, with two above and two below it.

Gulf flounder: three, large brown spots—one on rear part of lateral line, one above, and one below the lateral line just ahead of the middle of the body.

Groupers

Black grouper: dark, rectangular blotches on body, pectoral fin with a narrow, orange edge.

Gag: grayish body with wormlike marks and the first rays of the pelvic fins are whitish.

Yellowfin grouper: dark oval blotches on body and the outer third of the pectoral fin yellow.

Scamp: tan to gray-brown body with small, dark spots and fin rays extending beyond the rest of the fin on the soft dorsal, anal, and on the caudal fins, making it look somewhat feathered.

Red hind: red-brown spots on the body and the outer parts of the soft dorsal, anal, and caudal fins are blackish.

Nassau grouper: dark stripe through the eye with black dots around it, and a black saddle on the caudal peduncle.

Red grouper: reddish body and scarlet to orange mouth lining.

Warsaw grouper: dark brown body with ten dorsal spines, the second one longer than the rest.

Jewfish: tan with indistinct broad brown bands on the body and a rounded caudal fin.

Graysby: three or four white or dark spots along the base of the dorsal fin.

Yellowmouth grouper: tan to brown body and yellow inside of mouth.

Snappers

Distinguished from groupers by one or two enlarged canine teeth near the front of their jaws on both sides.

Cubera snapper: gray to purplish-brown and large.

Mangrove snapper: broad, dark stripe from tip of snout through the eye and almost to the dorsal fin.

Lane snapper: large, round dark spot below the soft dorsal fin and above the lateral line—also a caudal fin with a black edge.

Mutton snapper: olive to red body, blue streak below the eye, and a pointed anal fin.

Red snapper: back and upper sides scarlet to brick red, pointed anal fin, and a red iris.

Silk snapper: pinkish-red body, pointed anal fin, and a yellow iris.

Yellowtail snapper: a bright, yellow stripe starting at the tip of the snout and widening down the body until it colors the entire caudal fin.

Schoolmaster: brownish with eight pale vertical bars and a blue stripe below the eye.

Dog snapper: a series of blue dots and a white triangle below the eyes.

Mahogany snapper: a dark blotch on the lateral line and rounded anal fin.

Blackfin snapper: red body and head and a black blotch at the base of the pectoral fin.

Queen snapper: red body, very large eyes, and deeply forked caudal fin.

Vermilion snapper: pale red body with many short diagonal blue lines on the upper half of the body.

Tunas

Blackfin tuna: long pectoral fin, reaching almost to below the second dorsal fin.

Little tunny: wavy, dark stripes on the back and four to five dark spots below the pectoral fin.

Skipjack: three to five black stripes on the belly and sides.

Yellowfin tuna: a golden stripe on the side and long, yellow second dorsal and anal fins.

Atlantic bonito: seven or more dark oblique stripes on back.

Sharks

Blacktip shark: whitish stripe on the flank and black on the tip of the inside of the pectoral fin.

Hammerhead shark: very flat head expanded into lobes at its sides with eyes at the ends.

Tiger shark: blotches and tiger-like stripes on body and the upper lobe of the caudal fin is pointed.

Sand tiger shark: dark spots on body and both dorsal fins nearly equal in size.

Lemon shark: yellowish-brown body and both dorsal fins equally large.

Mako shark: bright blue to slate-blue back and white belly, slender body, and upper lobe of caudal fin pointing up less than 45 degrees.

Spinner shark: like the blacktip but the first dorsal fin begins above a point behind the pectoral fin.

Dusky shark: small first dorsal fin beginning above a point behind the pectoral fin.

Bull shark: large first dorsal fin beginning at a point above the middle of the pectoral fin.

Sandbar shark: distinguishable from the bull shark only by an expert.

Blacknose shark: dusky smudge at tip of the snout.

Nurse shark: barbel at the front edge of each nostril.

Bonnethead shark: similar to the hammerhead but the head more spade-shaped.

Silky shark: silky, smooth skin.

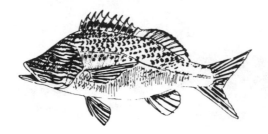

Grunts

White grunt: blue and yellow stripes on the head, blue spots on the body scales, and orange-red inside the mouth.

Margate: dark spot on each scale on the upper half of the body, inside of the mouth orange-red, and, with the exception of the pectoral, blackish fins.

Tomtate: yellow or bronze stripe from tip of snout to the base of the caudal fin, dark spot at the base of the caudal fin, and orange-red inside of mouth.

Spanish grunt: three dark stripes running down the body, yellow below the dorsal fin and on the caudal peduncle, and orange-red inside of mouth.

Cottonwick grunt: broad, black stripe from beginning of dorsal fins, widening as it goes, orange-red inside of mouth.

Sailor's choice: dark spots on scales form oblique rows and orange-red inside of mouth.

Bluestriped grunt: blue and bright yellow stripes from head to tail and orange-red inside of mouth.

Striped grunt: five dark stripes on body, caudal fin dark, and orange-red inside of mouth.

Pigfish: small mouth inside of which is not orange-red and a gray body with bronze and yellowish markings.

Porkfish: two large black bars on the head and front of body and the inside of mouth is not orange-red.

Jacks

Jack crevalle: steep head profile and a black area on the lower part of the pectoral fins.

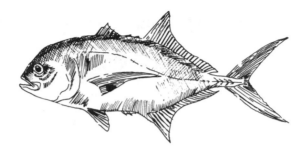

Horse-eye jack: rounded head profile and darkish hard part on caudal peduncle.

Yellow jack: yellow underneath body.

Blue runner: blue-green over entire back and a black spot on the edge of the gill plate.

Cottonmouth jack: milky-white inside of mouth and short pectoral fins.

Rainbow runner: blue, green, and yellow stripes on body and one dorsal and anal finlet.

African pompano: steep head profile and dorsal and anal fin rays extended in filaments.

Glossary

All-tackle record: In accordance with specific tackle criteria, the heaviest fish caught on hook and line as recorded by the International Game Fish Association (IGFA); in many cases larger specimens have been caught in other ways.

Barbels: Flesh appendages usually around the mouth.

Bottom structure: Sometimes called only structure, anything rising vertically from sea or bay bottom, such as reefs, wrecks, sunken material, rocks, etc.

Bow (to): Quickly lowering the rod tip and giving slack to a jumping or running fish.

Braided line: Woven fibers of nylon or Dacron that produce a fishing line suitable for certain trolling and casting purposes.

Chum: Materials such as whole live or dead fish, fish parts, ground-up fish and other ocean life, crushed sea shells, bread crumbs, oatmeal, etc.; any of these or a combination is put into the water to attract fish.

Continental Shelf: The sea bottom bordering continents that slopes downward from the coast and is 100 fathoms or less in depth; where it ends there is a sudden drop to 1,000 fathoms or more.

Conventional reel: a type of reel which collects line on a turning spool (compare with spinning reel).

Downrigger: A device to fish at a chosen depth that uses a heavy lead ball to pull the bait down in the water.

Dropback: The amount of time between a fish strike causing the clip to release the fishing line and when it becomes taut—an outrigger line has much dropback; a flat line has none.

Ebb tide: Outgoing tide.

Egg sinker: A weight shaped like an egg with a hole running through it for the fishing line—also called a slip or barrel sinker.

Flat line: Lines fished directly from the boat and not hoisted in the air (compare with outrigger line).

Flood tide: Incoming tide.

Freelining: Allowing a bait, alive or dead, to swim or float in the water with nothing on the line such as a weight or float to inhibit its movement.

Green fish: A fish not ready to be landed as it is still full of energy and possibly dangerous.

Gulf Stream: A great warm water current traveling north in the Atlantic Ocean off the coast of Florida.

High tide: The highest vertical point water reaches in its daily movement.

Horse (to): Bringing in a fish quickly, before it is exhausted.

Inshore: Close to the shorelines (compare with offshore).

Inside: Bodies of water such as bays, harbors, and inlets that are more or less protected by land from wind and wave.

Knock-down: When a striking fish pulls the fishing line out of the outrigger release clip.

Low tide: The lowest vertical point water reaches in its daily movement.

Mono: Monofilament fishing line, the type most often used.

Mudding: Bottom sediment stirred up by fish and/or shrimp.

Neap tide: Period of least tidal range occurring around the first and last quarters of the moon.

Offshore: Far from the shoreline.

Outrigger line: Lines suspended and fished from a point 20′ or so high and held there by a release clip attached to a line on a pulley which in turn runs along a long pole, the outrigger (compare with flat line).

Outside: Portion of a coastline where there is exposure to open water (compare with inside).

Planer: An inexpensive device designed to troll baits deep in the water.

Shock or shock leader: A short piece of heavy mono or wire linking hook to leader or tippet; it provides some insurance against the cutting of the line by fish with sharp teeth or rough scales and bodies.

Sight-fishing: Spotting a fish and casting to it.

Slack tide: When tidal movement is slow.

Slough: Deep areas in the surf running more or less parallel to the beach—also called a gut.

Spinning reel: A type of reel whose spool does not turn—on a cast, line comes off the spool in loops and on the retrieve, line is collected by an arm winding it back around the spool (compare with conventional reel).

Spring tide: Period of extreme tidal range occurring around the full and dark moon (has nothing to do with the time of year).

Stand: The time between the tides when there is no tidal flow.

Structure: See Bottom structure.

Swash canal: A narrow band of water in the surf running through and around sandbars out to sloughs and deeper water.

Tag line: A line attached at one end to a fixed object on a boat and the other, by means of a release clip, to either the outrigger or flat line.

Tailing: A feeding or swimming fish whose tail sticks up above the water's surface.

Teaser: A piece of colored wood, metal, or plastic, about a foot long, that trolled through the water makes a commotion—even a beverage can with holes punched in the ends qualifies.

Appendix G

For More Information

Books

Dunaway, Vic. *Baits, Rigs and Tackle.* Miami: Wickstrom Publishers, Inc., 1984. Just what its title says: a fine book with many illustrations.

Earp, Samuel A. and Wildeman, William J. *Secrets of Successful Big Game Fishing.* Boston: Little, Brown and Company, 1986. Excellent for descriptions and pictures of trolling rigs for the largest fishes.

Kreh, Lefty. *Fly Fishing in Salt Water.* New York: Nick Lyons Books, 1986. Necessary for any fly fisherman.

Kreh, Lefty. *Salt Water Fly Patterns.* Fullerton: Maral, Inc., 1989. For the saltwater fly fisherman, a necessity.

Robins, C. Richard and Ray, G. Carleton. *A Field Guide to Atlantic Coast Fishes.* Boston: Houghton Mifflin Co., 1986. The best book for identifying fishes in Florida; absolutely essential.

Sosin, Mark and Kreh, Lefty. *Fishing the Flats.* New York: Nick Lyons Books, 1983. A basic book for Florida flats fishing.

Soucie, Gary. *Hook, Line, and Sinker.* New York: Simon & Schuster Inc., 1988. An excellent reference book on terminal tackle.

Periodicals

Florida Sportsman Magazine. Wickstrom Publishers, Inc., Miami, Florida. The top fishing magazine for Florida saltwater fishing.
Salt Water Sportsman: Southern Edition. Times-Mirror Magazines, Boston, Massachusetts. The material on Florida is excellent.

Maps

Florida Sportsman Fishing Charts. Wickstrom Publishers, Inc. Miami, Florida.

Fishing Maps

The fishing maps are arranged so that they begin in northwest Florida, go south to the Keys, and then north along the Atlantic coast. Although fishes located on these maps are regularly caught where indicated, fishing in contiguous waters will be productive, as well. The coastline not mapped ranges from mediocre fishing near population centers to sensational where access is only by a long boat trip. Although the most sought-after species are indicated on the maps, many other varieties can also be found in each location. To more easily and readily orient yourself to the locations, use these maps with road maps and/or navigational charts. In no case should these maps be used for navigation purposes.

Use the following key for all maps:

A = amberjack	G = grunt	SN = snapper
B = barracuda	J = jack crevalle	S = snook
BD = black drum	K = king mackerel	SM = Spanish
BL = bluefish	L = ladyfish	mackerel
BM = blue marlin	P = permit	SB = striped bass
BN = bonefish	PM = pompano	T = tarpon
CM = cero mackerel	R = redfish	TT = tripletail
C = cobia	SL = sailfish	TU = tuna
D = dolphin	ST = seatrout	W = wahoo
F = flounder	SR = shark	WM = white marlin
GR = grouper	SH = sheepshead	WH = whiting

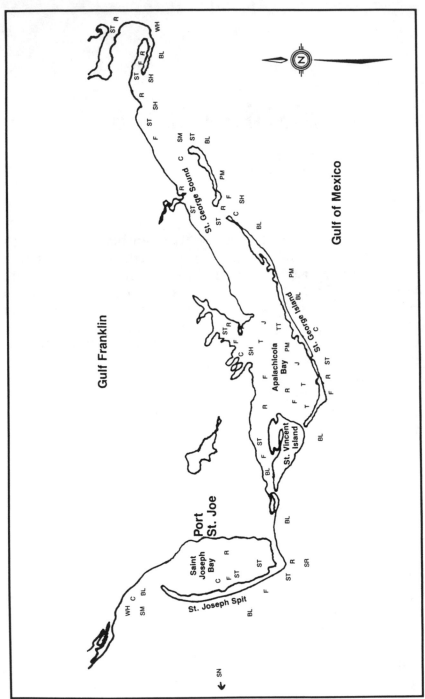

Area of Apalachicola

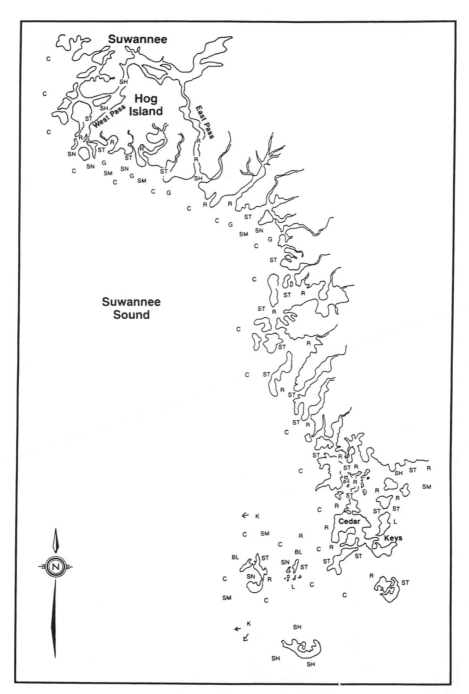

Suwannee to Cedar Keys

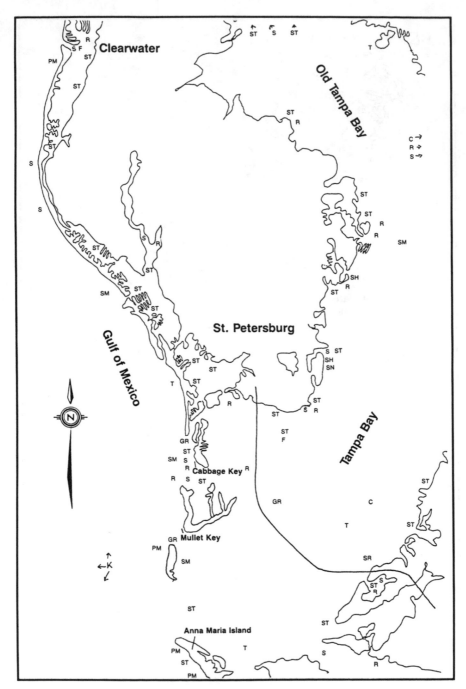

Tampa Bay

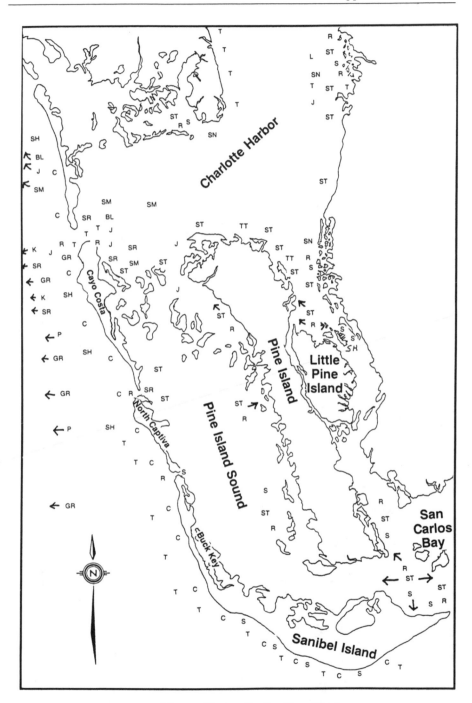

Boca Grande to Sanibel

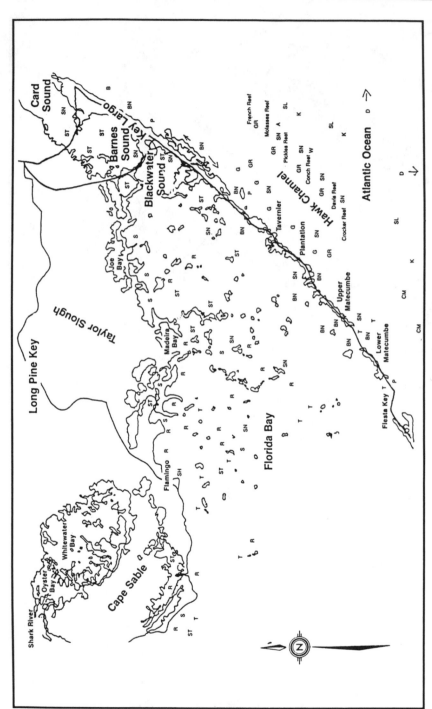

Florida Bay and Upper Keys

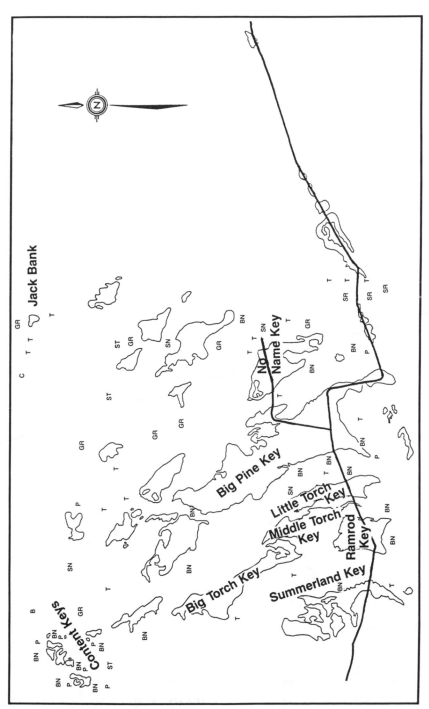

Big Pine Key area

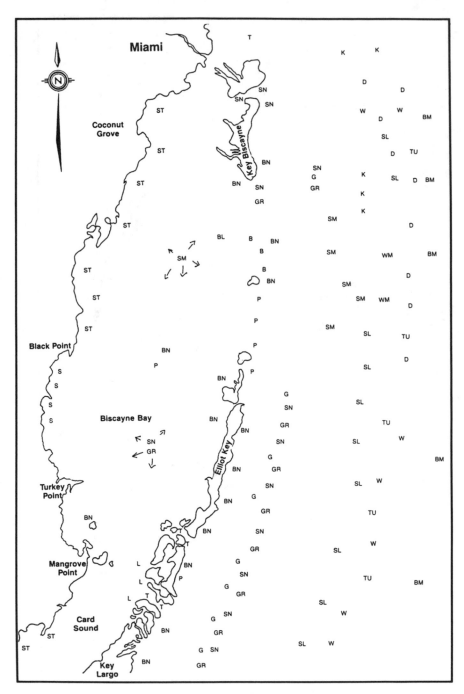

Biscayne Bay area

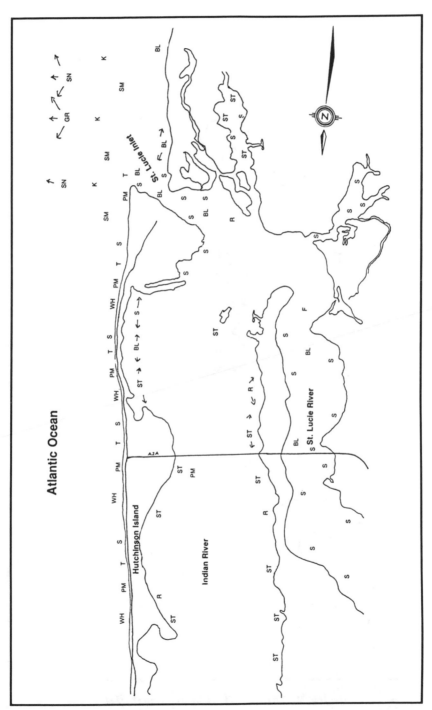

St. Lucie Inlet area

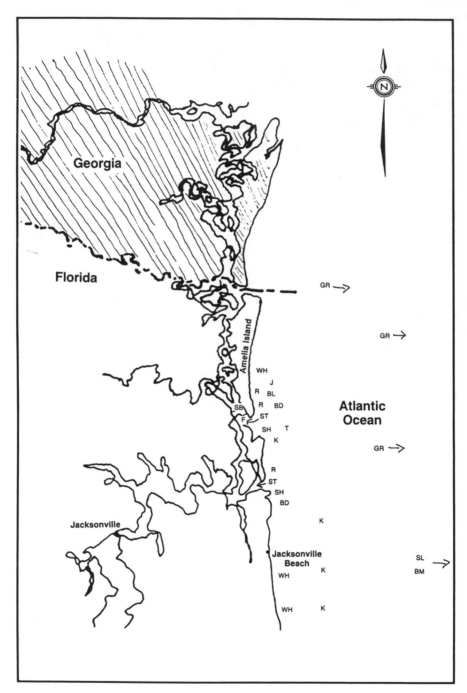

Jacksonville Beach to Georgia

Index